BETTER
NOT BIGGER

*How to Take Control of Urban Growth
and Improve Your Community*

Eben Fodor

NEW SOCIETY PUBLISHERS

Cataloguing in Publication Data:
A catalog record for this publication is available from the National
Library of Canada and the Library of Congress.

Cover design by David Lester, from photographs by Max Green and
Miriam MacPhail. The mural is painted on a wall in the East End of
Vancouver, B.C.

Printed in Canada on acid-free, partially recycled (20 percent post-
consumer) paper using soy-based inks by Transcontinental/Best Book
Manufacturers.

Paperback ISBN: 0-86571-386-3

Inquiries regarding requests to reprint all or part of *Better NOT Bigger*
should be addressed to New Society Publishers at the address below.

To order directly from the publishers, please add $4.00 shipping to the
price of the first copy, and $1.00 for each additional copy (plus GST in
Canada). Send check or money order to:

New Society Publishers
P.O. Box 189, Gabriola Island, B.C. V0R 1X0, Canada

New Society Publishers aims to publish books for fundamental social
change through nonviolent action. We focus especially on sustainable
living, progressive leadership, and educational and parenting
resources. Our full list of books can be browsed on the worldwide web
at: http://www.newsociety.com

NEW SOCIETY PUBLISHERS
Gabriola Island B.C., Canada and Stony Creek CT, U.S.A.

CONTENTS

WHERE ARE YOU

1. HOW MUCH MORE TRAFFIC CONGESTION WOULD YOU LIKE IN YOUR COMMUNITY?
   a) There is already plenty of traffic, thanks.
   b) Just a little bit more, please.
   c) A whole lot more.

2. HOW MUCH MORE AIR AND WATER POLLUTION WOULD YOU PREFER?
   a) We have too much already.
   b) Just a little more pollution, please.
   c) Give me toxic soup!

3. HOW MUCH MORE FARMLAND AND OPEN SPACE DO YOU WANT TO BE DEVELOPED?
   a) It would be nice if we could save what we have left.
   b) I suppose we have to sacrifice this land in the name of "progress."
   c) I can't bear the sight of undeveloped land going to waste.

4. HOW MUCH HIGHER DO YOU WANT YOUR TAXES TO GO?
   a) For what I'm getting, I think I'm paying enough already.
   b) I'm happy to pay more, even if I can't see any benefits.

ON THE GROWTH SPECTRUM?

5. *HOW MUCH MORE OF YOUR LOCAL NATURAL RESOURCES (FRESH WATER, ELECTRIC POWER SUPPLY, FORESTS, AGGREGATE AND MINERALS) DO YOU WANT CONSUMED?*

   a) I'd like to conserve our natural resources and use them as efficiently as possible.
   b) We have to sacrifice our resources to create prosperity.
   c) We should sell all our natural resources for a quick buck.

6. *WOULD YOU PREFER THAT YOUR CITY GOVERNMENT CONTINUE TO SUBSIDIZE NEW DEVELOPMENT, OR SHOULD THEY USE THE MONEY TO FUND SCHOOLS, EXTEND LIBRARY HOURS, OFFER DAY CARE AT COMMUNITY CENTERS, CREATE CULTURAL AND RECREATIONAL PRO-GRAMS, AND STILL HAVE ENOUGH LEFT OVER FOR A TAX CUT?*

   a) I'll take the expanded services and the tax cut, please.
   b) Let's keep the development fire stoked with my tax dollars.

7. *HOW MUCH BIGGER DO YOU WANT YOUR COMMUNITY TO BE?*

   a) It is already big enough.
   b) Let's just keep growing and see what happens!
   c) I love big cities, but am too lazy to move to one.

IF YOU ANSWERED "A" TO ONE OR MORE OF THESE QUESTIONS, THIS BOOK IS FOR YOU!

ACKNOWLEDGMENTS

Albert Bartlett has been a beacon of uncommon sense on growth, resource consumption and sustainability issues, and a major source of inspiration for this book. Many references to his insightful work have been included here. Dr. Bartlett is a popular speaker on population growth and energy and natural resource policy. He has generously given more than 1,300 presentations on these topics all over North America. In addition to his many published writings and his active role with several national and international organizations, Dr. Bartlett also finds time to make frequent contributions to his local newspaper in the form of commentary and letters to the editor on timely growth and urban planning issues.

I wish to thank Tom McKenna for sharing his extensive records spanning 25 years, on growth and development issues in Colorado and around the country. He provided many excellent references and case studies on the impacts of growth on communities, and abundant examples of the Urban Growth Machine in action.

Important contributions have been made to this book by a number of people through their reviews of one or more chapters, their contribution of resources, references and information, or through their sage advice. They include Mary Clark, John Baldwin, Tom Gries, Harvey Molotch, Stephen Burns, Susan Osborne, Dennis Lueck, Lynn Feekin, Alan Pittman, Erik Knoder, and Bill Boyer.

I wish to especially thank my partner, Koalani Roberts, for her good ideas, editing assistance and honest feedback that helped me successfully tackle some complex issues. Her contribution has made this book much more readable. Thanks finally to my father, Robert Fodor, mother, Folly King and step-father, John King, who contributed many helpful comments and suggestions. Their sense of balance and judgment improved the book substantially.

INTRODUCTION

*Growth is good, they say, reciting like an incantation the
prime article of faith of the official American religion: Bigger
is better and best is biggest. Growth, they tell us, means more
jobs, more bank accounts, more cars, more people, leading in
turn to the demand for more jobs, more economic expansion,
more industrial development. Where, when, and how is this
spiraling process supposed to reach a rational end — a state of
stability, sanity, and equilibrium?*

— Edward Abbey, *Learning to Listen to the Land*

A February 5, 1998 article appearing in a major Oregon newspaper was headlined: "Inevitable growth worries small towns."
The article reported that 13 of 16 communities in southern
Oregon "have expressed a desire to remain small towns, but growth is
inevitable." Residents are concerned that growth will destroy the character of their communities and cause them to merge together in a
"seamless" mass of urban development — and they feel powerless to
do anything about it.

In these circumstances, the standard refrain of many public officials is that "growth is a given." It's not a question of *whether* we'll grow,
they say, but *how*. This sort of resignation that growth is inevitable is
simplistic at best. At worst, it shows a callous attitude toward the legitimate concerns of citizens and a reckless disregard for the long-term
consequences of endless urban growth.

As a citizen who is wondering about the effects of growth on your community, you undoubtedly have many unanswered questions. You may find yourself asking: Is continued growth really desirable? Are the benefits attributed to growth realistic? Have all the costs been accounted for? If growth were found to be undesirable, would we be able to stop it? If we were able to stop growth, what would the alternatives look like?

To some extent, the answers lie in uncharted territory. We have accepted the necessity of growth in such an unquestioning manner that there has been little serious consideration of growth alternatives. There is an astonishing lack of good information about the real impacts of growth on our communities. There is very little awareness of the strategies and policy options for slowing or limiting growth. And good role models for stable communities are hard to find.

This book is intended to be a resource for individuals and groups who want to get off the treadmill of urban growth. It provides insights, ideas, information, tools, and techniques to make the transition away from growth-oriented and growth-addicted communities and toward stability. This book brings together some of the best available information on these topics. It is written for those who are seeking a more balanced, informed and productive discussion about growth. Overall, the message is intended to be one of optimism and empowerment. Responsible policies toward growth will foster strong, healthy communities that will remain great places to live for generations to come.

This book grew out of my own involvement in community growth issues and my frustration with the lack of good information about the real impacts of urban growth and the apparent lack of good policy options. In an effort to answer my own questions about this fascinating and complex subject, I have found many contradictions and surprising insights. I have uncovered excellent resources and references from all over North America. And I have found that effective policy options for curbing growth do exist.

IS GROWTH MAKING YOUR COMMUNITY BETTER OR JUST BIGGER?

My family's farm in rural Maryland was a wonderful place to grow up. As a kid roaming Nature's playground, I formed a strong bond with the land and fell in love with the beautiful rural landscape of rolling hills and valleys covered with pastures, cornfields, streams, and woods. The wide-open spaces, fresh breezes, and deep quiet of nature at work provided a constant source of pleasure and refreshment. Sometimes we rode our horses on the lightly traveled rural roads that were as likely to carry a tractor as a car. Crime was unheard of, doors were never locked, and we could go for five years without even seeing a police car.

Our family farm is still much the same as it was in my childhood. But the surrounding hills and valleys are now covered by "view homes" on five-acre lots. There is only one other farm left nearby — a dairy farmer — and he will be gone soon. The dirt roads that had served people well for two and a half centuries became too dusty for the heavy traffic and were paved. The neighbors drive great distances for the privilege of living in this "rural" environment. Many spend three to four hours a day commuting to and from work in, or near, Washington, D.C. The Interstate 270 route to the District was a brand new four-lane highway when I was a kid. Now, its 14 lanes are routinely filled with bumper-to-bumper traffic stretching ten or 20 miles.

As a witness to this transformation of the landscape, I have a sense of tragic loss. No future generation will enjoy what I had. But other communities have seen far worse. This scenario of urbanization has repeated itself a thousand times in a thousand places.

Most of the physical changes resulting from urban expansion are permanent. We make irreversible commitments of resources — land, energy, and water. We create social and environmental impacts on the existing community. And we incur economic costs, many of which are not paid by the new development itself. Urban growth often has profoundly negative impacts on the existing community. Yet we hear that growth will provide us with benefits that offset these impacts. And we hear that even if we wanted to slow, or stop growth, there is little we can do.

Our cities and towns keep growing and growing. "To what end?" you might ask. Are big cities so much better than small cities that we should strive to convert every small city into a bigger one? It seems clear from looking at many of the world's largest cities that we have little reason to envy them. Maybe there is some ideal size where all the best qualities of a community come together to reach an optimal state of urban harmony? If there is such a size, would we know when we've reached it? Would we be able to stop growing once we were there? The reality is that we just grow and grow, regardless of our community's size or whether further growth is good or bad for us. Endless growth is the only plan on the table.

There are certainly benefits associated with urban growth. At a minimum, it produces a temporary income to those associated with the development — the developers, contractors, and construction workers. Other beneficiaries of development may include the sellers of the land, realtors, lawyers, bankers, and so forth. The public may enjoy some benefits too from the increased diversity growth brings. There will be more shopping opportunities, more restaurants, and more movie theaters. Growth may also bring individuals with new ideas and talents who enhance the life of the community. But how high are the costs we pay in exchange for these benefits?

Understanding the Urban Growth Machine

One reason local efforts to control growth have not been more successful is a failure to recognize the influence of the urban growth industry. Powered by common economic interests, this group of businesses works together like a machine to perpetuate growth and divert local resources to accommodate growth. As you will see in Chapter 2, the urban growth machine is a fixture in many communities and often becomes a powerful force in local politics. It funds candidates for city council, fights citizen ballot measures, and runs public relations campaigns. Where growth machines are well-entrenched, citizens may face major barriers to change on growth issues.

Many of our local governments are on a growth "autopilot." Citizens seeking responsiveness and accountability from their governments find that there doesn't appear to be anyone at the controls. These governments have become a part of the growth machine whose primary function is to build roads and infrastructure and to provide development services for an ever-expanding mass of subdivisions, industrial parks, and shopping centers.

The influence of the growth machine often produces public policies that benefit a select few at the expense of the rest of the community. One result of such policies is an increasing number of citizens who are dissatisfied with their government. This dissatisfaction has manifested itself in citizen tax revolts all across the U.S. Two decades of rapid growth in California led up to the passage of the famous Proposition 13 in 1978 that slashed revenues for local governments and dropped that state's school system from one of the best in the U.S. to the bottom of the pack. Many other fast-growing states have faced similar anti-government tax reforms.

The solution, described in Chapter 2, is to get the growth machine out of local government and to enact the kinds of reforms that keep it out. These reforms build on the principles of a democratic government that serves the general public interest over narrow special interests. Switching off the growth machine requires a truly representative local government and active public participation in local land use issues.

You can help switch off the growth machine simply by becoming informed and active in your community.

UNCOVERING THE BIG MYTHS ABOUT GROWTH

How much is urban growth really linked with economic growth and prosperity? Does urban growth foster economic growth or is it the other way around? Can we have a prosperous local economy without urban growth? What is the relationship between population growth and urban growth? Do the benefits of continued growth outweigh the costs? These are important questions our society is only just beginning to address.

We will start to answer some of these questions by shattering the myths surrounding growth and its relationships with jobs, housing, and economic prosperity. Growth issues are often highly distorted by platitudes about the alleged benefits of growth or the dire consequences of not growing. We can debunk the growth mythology with facts, logic, and common sense. Good decisions about growth start with good information.

There is what can only be called a giant *public relations campaign* being waged in our cities, counties, and states. This campaign is primarily the work of the real estate development industry — the engine of the urban growth machine — that doesn't want you to question the benefits of continued growth nor be aware of the costs it creates. The development industry's public relations efforts have resulted in a great deal of confusion, inaccurate information, and empty rhetoric about growth. The rhetoric includes statements like: "Growth creates jobs," "You have to grow or die," "Growth generates new tax revenues," and many more. As you will see in Chapter 3, such statements have fundamental flaws in the context of urban growth. These kinds of statements must be evaluated more critically and many should be rejected outright.

Right now, the development industry is at work in Oregon, and possibly your state or province too, trying to convince policymakers that growth controls will have negative effects on housing affordability, and therefore should be abandoned. They have found the affordable housing issue to be a convenient pry bar to take apart existing growth controls and fend off new ones. The public's penchant for good jobs has been used as a similar excuse for perpetuating growth. Both the jobs and the housing issues — involving two of the biggest growth myths — are addressed in more detail in Chapter 4.

How Much is Growth Costing You?

When I first issued my study, "The Real Cost of Growth in Oregon," in July 1996, it was greeted with excitement by many citizens who were eager for credible information on growth impacts. I sold hundreds of copies across the U.S. and eventually published it in the journal *Population and Environment.* But the business community in Oregon greeted the report with disdain, skepticism, and worse. The report summarized the professional and academic literature on the cost of growth and calculated an approximate cost for providing public facilities to a single new house at $24,500. At first, newspapers refused to print the findings. Various homebuilder associations around the state viewed the report as a mean-spirited attack on their industry and did their best to discredit the study and its author in editorials, letters to the editor, and even paid advertisements. But as more attention is given to growth costs, the study's conclusions are being confirmed.

The "Cost of Growth" study was done with very limited resources (my own!), and the report was never intended to be the final word on growth costs. Rather, it was meant to show that urban growth does involve real net costs to the community, that these costs can be quantified, and that they are quite high. (Much of this information is reported in Chapter 5). I had hoped to encourage local governments to analyze growth-related costs and provide the public with better information about how growth is impacting their communities.

The response has been slow, but it seems to be taking effect in Oregon and elsewhere. Portland has just begun to take its first close look at growth-related costs. Oregon's governor convened a task force to examine the fiscal impacts of growth statewide. In the two years since my study was done, I have continued researching the literature on growth costs and have collected many more references from all over the country. The findings of municipal reports, academic literature, and professional studies over the past 25 years are generally consistent with those in my original report.

As you will see in the chapters that follow, the high costs of growth are well documented. This is in spite of the surprising fact that the fiscal impacts of growth remain one of the most understudied aspects of our economy. A researcher in this field might conclude that there is a vast conspiracy of intentional ignorance at work. How else can one explain the apparent lack of concern for how billions of hard-earned tax dollars are spent every year?

City officials often tell us that growth is good for us, that it will increase our tax base, and provide needed jobs. But what is the benefit of a bigger tax base if growth places even greater demands on the tax base than it contributes? And what is the benefit of more jobs if the act of creating those jobs attracts more people to the community seeking work than there are jobs to be filled? The evidence of past growth tells us that the net result of growth is to increase the local tax burden and to produce a larger population that has even more unemployed people than before. How can we continue to count these as benefits when they are more often liabilities?

The municipal cost-benefit balance sheet on urban growth rarely has anything listed in the "costs" column. While the new tax revenues resulting from growth are tallied, the associated costs of expanding pubic facilities and services are ignored. If a private company had a business plan that looked only at revenues and ignored costs, it would quickly be out of business. Why should the public tolerate such one-sided accounting by local governments? We make tremendous expenditures of public resources to support growth, yet fail to account for these costs in terms of the impact on existing residents and taxpayers.

When we fully understand the social, environmental, and economic costs of growth, it should be clear to everyone that there are advantages to controlling growth. This book summarizes the best available information on the cost of growth and provides tips for estimating the real cost of growth in your community.

FINDING THE RIGHT GROWTH CONTROLS FOR YOUR COMMUNITY

While surveys reveal that most people are skeptical about the benefits of further growth, an entirely different conclusion seems to have been reached by policymakers in most communities. These policymakers have concluded that citizens want more growth, and they want it so badly it should be publically subsidized at taxpayers' expense. Urban growth is publically subsidized in at least ten different ways in cities throughout the U.S. The result of this subsidization is that we have the growth accelerator pedal pushed firmly to the floor. Those who say there is nothing we can do to slow growth fail to recognize or acknowledge that we are actively encouraging it. Chapter 6 describes how growth is being encouraged and suggests growth-neutral policies to remove growth subsidies and incentives.

Growth problems are rearing their heads at increasing rates in communities across the U.S. Many of these communities are realizing that it is no longer merely a question of how to grow but *whether* to grow. Instead of *smarter* growth these communities want *less* growth. Civic leaders, environmentalists, astute planners, and public officials all over North America are looking for that perfect community that has solved its growth problems. But the Shangri-la of growth management eludes us. We haven't yet created this model community that has successfully addressed growth in a responsible, long-term manner.

There are, however, many effective strategies in use today that will moderate or restrict growth in desirable ways. These strategies can directly reduce the negative impacts of growth and preserve the quality and character of a community. An extensive collection of proven growth controls and case studies are described in Chapter 6. The emphasis here is on those policies that will actually slow growth in your community. Keep in mind that these growth controls are still a relatively new area in public policy and techniques are still evolving.

CREATE A BETTER COMMUNITY

Can slowing growth actually improve your community? The answer is a resounding "Yes!" By controlling growth, communities can take charge of their future. Stable, sustainable communities have the potential to reach new heights in virtually every area of community endeavor. These include opportunities to:

- improve local quality of life;
- improve public services (without new taxes);
- maintain or improve environmental quality;
- protect local agricultural and resource lands;
- preserve the community's cultural and historic heritage; and
- provide economic security and well-being for all residents.

It is not a question of whether we should have stable, sustainable communities, but when and how. Our choice is between either a community that grows until it is ultimately forced to stop by intolerable conditions, or a community that takes charge of its own destiny by identifying an ideal or optimal population size and setting goals towards reaching and maintaining that size. It is undoubtedly easier to obtain an optimal size by starting sooner rather than later.

The stable, sustainable community offers intriguing possibilities. Far from being a place where people are poor, life is dull, and nothing changes, the stable community is likely to be strong, dynamic, and prosperous. Individual liberties should be greater, not fewer. The local economy can operate more efficiently without the constant turmoil of expansion. Employment levels may be higher and local government can provide better services that cost less.

Better NOT Bigger provides convenient access to the broad range of information and ideas citizens need in order to be effective participants in the urban growth debate. The information is practical and includes many useful concepts and insights. Growth issues and solutions are illustrated with case studies from around the U.S. Helpful references and resources are provided in the appendices. For some people, this book may validate much of what they have personally observed about urban growth, but could not confirm from other sources.

I hope that every reader concludes this book with a strong sense of optimism about the future of their community as it enters the new millennium. And I hope that you will take with you, into your next city council or neighborhood meeting, some new ideas about how to solve the nagging problems of urban growth and make your community a *better* place to live.

THE
ENDANGERED LANDSCAPE

*All ethics ... rest upon a single premise: that the individual is a
member of a community of interdependent parts... The land ethic
simply enlarges the boundaries of the community to include
soils, waters, plants and animals, or collectively: the land...*

*A land ethic then, reflects the existence of an ecological con-
science, and this in turn reflects a conviction of individual
responsibility for the health of the land. Health is the capacity
of the land for self-renewal. Conservation is our effort to
understand and preserve this capacity.*

— Aldo Leopold, *A Sand County Almanac*

GROWTH ON SEATTLE'S FRONT PORCH

Seattle has been among the nation's fastest growing cities and has
seen more than its share of sprawling growth pressures over the
past 20 years. In the 1980s the surrounding King County population rose 18.7 percent and development consumed land at an even
faster rate. To help control sprawling growth, the state legislature
passed the Growth Management Act in 1990, which requires comprehensive planning and urban growth boundaries. The city has recently
started tackling its transportation and housing problems with
neighborhood-based planning and investment.

In an impressive example of civic journalism, *The Seattle Times* teamed with the local public radio and TV stations to sponsor a series of public forums on growth issues in the Seattle-Tacoma-Everett area called the "Front Porch Forum."[1] One part of this series was a mock citizen trial of local growth policies. "Had the region done enough to protect the area's treasured quality of life?" the jury was asked.

A panel of local officials and organizations served as witnesses and described the many programs and policies being used to manage the region's growth. But the diverse, 97-member citizen jury was not placated by these speakers.

The citizen jury ruled that the region's leaders (and its citizens) were "guilty" of failing to take adequate action to protect the area's quality of life in the face of growth. According to one observer, anger, frustration, and despair were chief among the sentiments expressed. Many did not want to "manage" growth, they wanted to stop it. "But everyone assumes that growth is a given," the observer noted.

According to the *Times*, many spoke of gaining nothing from the economic boom that has spurred the region's recent growth spurt. Instead, they talked about rising rents and housing prices they and their children can't afford. In addition to problems with traffic and sprawling land use patterns, they spoke of a diminishing sense of community and a growing alienation from government. "If growth means nothing to most people but higher living costs, more traffic, and a stressed environment, then why pursue it?" some asked.

COMMUNITIES AT RISK

Growth, especially rapid growth, can leave communities permanently scarred, deeply in debt, and drowning in traffic, with unaffordable housing, a lost sense of community, and a sacrificed environmental quality. Many communities will never recover from the impacts of rapid growth.

The same scenario plays out again and again. Once-friendly neighborhoods have their streets transformed into commuter corridors for a nearby 500-unit subdivision. Noise and traffic hazards make these older neighborhoods less livable. Open space disappears and existing parks become overcrowded. Quality of life declines while crime rates, local taxes, and the cost of living all go up.

The pressures and demands of growth divert community resources away from providing basic public services. Schools, libraries, and other public facilities become overcrowded. Angry voters refuse to support new bonds and levies and instead slash government funding.

Underfunded local governments that fail to identify the real costs of growth risk further incurring the anger of voters who wonder why they are getting so little for their tax dollars.

A community destroyed by growth may also lose its strongest supporters — the community leaders who no longer have anything to protect and the families who decide that their dreams of a good community must lie somewhere else. Community vision fades before a future of endless growth.

THE CHANGING LANDSCAPE

A sustainable society has been defined as one that meets the needs of the present without compromising the ability of future generations to meet their own needs.[2] But it's not hard to see that much of our natural inheritance is slipping through our fingers. Each day we have less to pass on to the next generation. In the U.S., we have lost 95 percent of our old-growth forests, 55 percent of our wetlands, and 99 percent of our native prairies. During our short lives, most of us have witnessed an unprecedented transformation of the landscape. Urban development in North America has covered more land in the last 50 years than in all previous history. Between 1982 and 1992, 14 million acres of the U.S. became developed land.[3] This area of newly urbanized land is equal in size to football fields laid end-to-end circling the earth nine times. Urban sprawl in the U.S. is consuming 160 acres of land every hour.

Each new office park, shopping mall, subdivision, paved road, or parking lot removes one more increment of land from Nature's inventory of natural habitats and healthy watersheds. We lose ecological diversity and weaken Nature's ability to assimilate our pollution. The result is a steady erosion of the integrity of the natural environment.

Armed with bulldozers, backhoes, dump trucks, concrete mixers, nail guns, and power saws, we are expanding our *built environment* at ever-increasing rates. Woods and grasslands have succumbed to the unrelenting stampede of urbanization. Our cornfields have become shopping malls and our forested hilltops have become subdivisions. Nature is beating a fast retreat before this onslaught.

The Earth's total biological productivity as a result of photosynthesis is measured as the net primary productivity (NPP). This is the net production by primary producers (plants) from solar energy and represents the potential food source for all other consumers not capable of photosynthesis. According to one estimate,[4] humans are now using 40 percent of the Earth's terrestrial NPP. The remaining 60 percent is what

THE CHANGING LANDSCAPE

We have been the most prodigal of people with land, and for years we wasted it with impunity. There was so much of it, and no matter how we fouled it, there was always more over the next hill, or so it seemed.

— William H. Whyte, *The Last Landscape*

is available to all other land-based species. As our share of the NPP pie grows, we literally push other species off the planet. Rates of extinction have increased far beyond natural levels with an estimated 27,000 species disappearing every year.[5]

As the saying goes, "We are what we eat." Most of the food that makes up our bodies comes directly or indirectly from the soil. The fruits, nuts, grains, and vegetables that keep us alive are direct products of dirt. The meats we eat are usually just one step along the food chain. Our drinking water runs over the surface of the earth or seeps through underground aquifers. When we recognize how close our link is to the soil, it is clear that the health of the land is directly tied to the health of those who live on it. We cannot mistreat our land without mistreating ourselves in some way. We might escape the consequences of poor land use for a while, but they will catch up with us eventually.

From space, our satellites have a clear view of what's going on. A growing world population is facing a shrinking agricultural land base. Surprisingly, digital satellite data are only just beginning to be analyzed to determine how our planet's land resources are being impacted by humans. Preliminary indications are that most of our urban areas have been built on the best farming soils. The practice of siting new development on our best farmland continues. California is losing its incredibly productive agricultural land to development at a rate of 100,000 acres a year. At the current rate of loss, approximately half of California's cropland will no longer be available for production in less than 20 years.[6] Nationally, the loss of agricultural land in the U.S. is approaching half a million acres every year. At this rate we will lose an area of productive farmland larger than the state of Maryland every 20 years — enough arable land to feed 30 million people.

Urbanization is the most alarming of our land use trends because growing cities and towns consume land so rapidly. This growth permanently destroys many of the productive values of natural land: food production potential; outdoor recreation opportunities; open space; fresh air; quiet and serenity; beautiful views; watershed quality (water purification, groundwater recharging, and flood control); wildlife habitat; species diversity; and ecosystem functions. Most of these values are not reflected in the market price of land as a commodity. All of these values are likely to be much greater to future generations than they are to the current generation.

The process of urbanization is, in any practical sense, irreversible. Typically, raw land is divided into small building lots (four to eight housing sites per acre). The natural land contours are destroyed by bulldozers. Utilities are buried in the ground. Streets and sidewalks are paved. House foundations are excavated. Concrete is poured for footings and driveways. And finally, many tons of resources (bricks, wood, metal, glass, plastics, asphalts, paints, and other materials) are committed to constructing the houses. Shopping centers and commercial developments follow the housing. There is little likelihood that such urbanization will ever be removed and the land restored to its natural state.

> **GONE WITH THE WIND**
>
> *Land is the only thing in the world that amounts to anything, for 'tis the only thing in this world that lasts .... 'Tis the only thing worth working for, worth fighting for – worth dying for.*
>
> — Gerald O'Hara, in *Gone with the Wind*, by Margaret Mitchell

ALL GROWTH IS NOT THE SAME

The term "growth" can mean many things. One person might say that growth of the economy is good, while another says that urban growth is bad. They are talking about distinctly different kinds of growth and we must begin to separate them in our thinking about growth issues.

Because there are many different types of growth, it's a good idea to start off by clarifying which types we are, and are not, addressing here. We are not focusing on personal, spiritual, intellectual, or emotional growth. We are not necessarily addressing growth of economic well-being, prosperity, equity, or security. All these kinds of growth can be quite beneficial.

The subject of this book is *urban* growth — the quantitative increase in the size of the urban "built" environment. When the term "growth" is used alone in this book it will be referring to urban growth. The distinction is intended to show that it is possible for our social and economic condition to continue to improve and for our human potential to grow, even while our urban areas do not.

From an ecological perspective, all of life exists in a finite world with finite resources. In a finite world, growth can be: part of a cyclical phenomenon (such as the change in seasons), which is accompanied

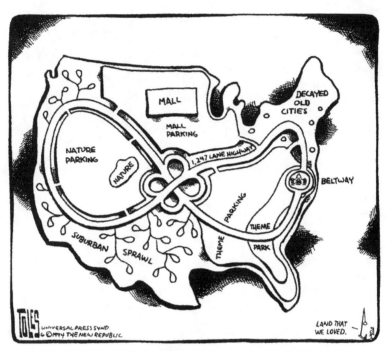

by death; a short-term response to a natural disturbance (fire, flood, storm, disease, etc.) which involves the replacement of the former biota with a new set; or a displacement of one or more species by another. There is no net growth in the biota. Instead, one life replaces or displaces another. There is a balance in Earth's life-supporting capacity that remains relatively constant. Ecologically, growth is a temporary phenomenon. All populations will eventually stop growing, and so must we, but who can say at what point that will occur? If we were somehow able to grow to the point where humans were utilizing every available ecological niche on the planet for our own needs, then we would be living on a very lonely and sterile planet.

ROOT CAUSES OF URBAN GROWTH

Urban growth often goes hand in hand with population growth. However this link is not quite as clear as one might assume. Urban growth is commonly thought to be the simple result of local population growth. But much of the construction of buildings, roads, and public facilities involved in urban growth actually takes place *in anticipation* of future population growth. This anticipation of growth includes the extra capacity we build into new roads, sewage treatment plants, and so forth. It also includes the speculative development that occurs with the assumption that continued growth will generate new buyers or tenants for the property. As a result, there are many cases where urban growth will actually precede, and even drive, local population growth.

Some people may think that to slow urban growth in their community, they first have to slow the natural rate of population growth, a daunting and unpopular task. But that is not entirely correct. Urban growth is certainly a consequence of population growth and, ultimately, stable communities will require stable population levels. But urban growth in your community is also a consequence of two other factors: *expanding consumption levels* and *in-migration* from other communities.

Our per-capita consumption of housing continues to increase. Between 1970 and 1990 the population of the U.S. increased at a rate of about one percent a year (see Figure 1-1). But the number of housing units increased at twice that rate — about two percent per year. If this growth rate continues, we will double the total amount of housing in the U.S. every 35 years.

Over the same period (1970–1990), the size of the average new home increased from 1,500 square feet to more than 2,000 square feet while the average number of persons in each house declined from 3.1 to 2.6. Each year we are building bigger houses for fewer occupants and using more resources per person than ever before.

The data in Figure 1-1 show us that new home construction is only half driven by population growth. The other half is driven by our expanding levels of housing *consumption*.

Figure 1-1
Changes in Population and Housing, U.S.

Characteristic	1970	1990	Percent Change 1970-1990
Population	203,302,031	248,718,291	22%
Number of Households	63,401,000	93,347,000	47%
Avg. Household Size (persons)	3.14	2.63	-16%
Avg. New House Size (sq. ft.)	1,500	2,080	39%

Source: U.S. Bureau of the Census: Statistical Abstract of the United States, 1995.

Urban Growth = Increasing Population + Increasing Consumption Levels

Urban development is consuming more land per capita than it once did. On average, each person in the U.S. requires approximately one acre of developed land for urbanization, industrial spread, and transportation systems.[7] About half of the land consumed in this manner is arable. Between 1970 and 1990 Chicago's population grew by only four percent, but the land area used by that population increased 46 percent. Los Angeles increased its population by 45 percent over the same period, but expanded its land area by 300 percent.[8]

Increasing automobile usage also contributes to urban growth. Twenty-five percent or more of the urban land area is devoted to auto travel. From 1969 to 1990, the number of vehicles increased six times faster than U.S. population. Vehicle miles traveled per person increased 51 percent from 3.9 miles to 5.9 miles.[9]

The average North American citizen consumes five times as many resources as the average world citizen. Since most of the resources we use come from outside our cities, each North American is actually impacting a much larger area than just the land they live on. Mathis Wackernagel and William Rees have developed the concept of an "ecological footprint" for urban areas to foster an understanding of the combined population and consumption impacts on the environment.[10] The ecological footprint includes the land area needed to provide food, housing, transportation, waste absorption, consumer goods and services to each person. On average, each North American requires 11 to 13 acres of ecologically productive land to supply his/her current consumption levels. By contrast, the average resident of India has an ecological footprint of only one acre. If everyone on Earth had the same levels of consumption as North Americans, we would need *three planets* to satisfy our demands.

Local population growth has two components: the natural increase in the existing population (births minus deaths), and the *in-migration* of new residents. In-migration is the flow of people into an area from other parts of the country. It is what produces the extremely high rates of growth we have seen in some cities and regions. While the total U.S. population has grown at an average rate of one percent a year, many communities see annual population growth rates of three, four, five, six, and even seven percent. Such rates of growth are the result of people relocating to take advantage of benefits they perceive from living in that community.

It is possible to influence both consumption and in-migration levels in your community without first resolving the issue of natural population growth at the local, national, or global level. As more and more communities adopt policies to slow or limit their growth, it will become more evident that the natural increase in local population must also be addressed. For now, there are ample opportunities to control urban growth before solutions to population growth are implemented.

REGULATING LAND USE

Americans are still debating the precise meaning of land ownership. Property-rights advocates say that ownership conveys the right to use the land in whatever manner suits the owner. But ownership of land has never been a firm concept involving a fixed set of rights. In fact, it is only through government regulation that land can be owned in the first place. Yet, property-rights advocates complain bitterly that government is taking away their vested rights. They say that regulations chip away at their ability to put the land to its most profitable uses. There have been many recent attempts in federal and state legislatures to force governments to compensate landowners for any loss in value that is caused by a new regulation. But most land regulations provide protections and benefits to *all* landowners. Good regulations *enhance* property values. We ban pig farms in residential neighborhoods so homeowners don't have to put up with noxious odors and farmers don't have to listen to the complaints. Everyone benefits — both land uses are more profitable when they don't conflict with each other. Occasionally regulations do have the impact of lowering some property values. Good land regulations should always create far more public benefits than private costs. If they don't, the particular regulation may be at fault, not the entire concept of land use regulation.

Land use regulation is not just a black-and-white issue, as it is often painted by the media. Whenever a new regulation will cause a significant hardship or reduction in values for a property owner, the government should, and usually does, consider ways to compensate the owner. This may include re-imbursing the owner for diminished values or buying the land outright at fair market value. The benefits the public receives from a particular regulation may warrant this expense. If not, perhaps the regulation is not needed or is poorly crafted.

THE SOLUTION TO SPRAWL

There is increasing recognition that keeping urban areas compact is better than allowing scattered or low-density sprawling development.

We abuse land because we regard it as a commodity belonging to us. When we see land as a community to which we belong, we may begin to use it with love and respect.

— Aldo Leopold in *The Quiet Crisis*, Stewart Udall

By channeling new growth to existing urban areas we reduce our footprint on the landscape and preserve open space, wildlife habitat, and resource lands — and save money on public facilities too. When given the choice between sprawling onto rural lands or holding the line through urban growth boundaries or other means, citizens usually choose to hold the line against sprawl. But the choice is not an easy one, because increased urban density can threaten the quality of life enjoyed by existing residents.

Oregon's cities have 25 years of experience controlling sprawl with urban growth boundaries. In Portland, polls show that residents strongly favor holding the line on sprawl, even when this results in increased density. But the city has faced growing criticism about policies intended to avoid sprawl by encouraging higher density development, infill, and redevelopment. The mayor of Milwakie, a Portland suburb, along with two city councilors were recently recalled by voters who didn't like their support of these policies. What is the message when people don't want sprawling development, but don't want density either? Could it be they want to keep things the way they are and preserve what they have? Perhaps they are simply saying, "We don't want more growth."

Urban planners and policy-makers have been hesitant to acknowledge the widely held sentiments favoring slower growth. Instead we hear rhetorical answers like "you can't stop growth" and "growth controls don't work." Citizens who accept these answers are once again left with the same unpleasant choices: grow out or grow up. And the planners go back to work figuring out how to accommodate more growth while minimizing its negative impacts on communities and rural lands.

But who is to say that slowing growth is not a viable option? The fact is that we have much to learn about the potential for controlling growth. There is little published research on the effectiveness of urban growth controls. No nationwide study of growth controls has ever been performed. The few localized studies that exist are far from comprehensive. What's more, the studies that do exist reach differing conclusions. Some say that growth controls are effective while others say they are not. These few studies are clearly no basis for dismissing an important third option for communities facing tough growth pressures: slowing or limiting growth.

In addition to the lack of a definitive analysis of growth controls, we lack practical experience with such policies. Only a handful of communities have applied growth controls in a comprehensive, systematic way. As described in this book, there are examples where these policies have been successfully implemented, have been well received by the public and appear to be achieving their goals. Unfortunately, there are also examples of poorly conceived and poorly implemented growth controls.

Many potential growth controls, and combinations of controls, are still waiting to be put to use. Among these, my personal favorites are *growth threshold standards*. These standards offer communities a means of holding the line on local quality of life. By setting threshold standards for growth, communities can protect the environmental, social, and economic qualities they value. As described in Chapter 6, communities can set standards for air quality, traffic congestion, school classroom size, or any other quality threatened by growth.

Smart Growth versus Less Growth

There are two distinctly different, but completely compatible and even complementary, approaches to growth management. One is concerned with *how* growth should occur. The other is concerned with *whether* growth should occur. Both approaches should be part of a responsible, long-term growth management program.

The approach that focuses on *how* growth occurs is sometimes referred to as *planned growth* or *smart growth*. The general strategy here is to influence the quality of growth and to minimize its negative effects. Planned growth uses a variety of techniques to direct new development in ways that will reduce the negative impacts on resource lands, environmental quality, livability, taxes, and other key qualities of our communities. Planned growth seeks to anticipate and accommodate growth through a comprehensive planning and policy framework. Most of the growth management practiced today fits into this category. However, this approach fails to address the amount of growth that is desirable.

The second approach to growth management focuses on *whether* growth should occur, and, if so, how much and how fast. This approach might be referred to as *finite-world planning*. It recognizes limits to growth and makes the reasonable assumption that our communities cannot grow forever. It supposes that we may be able to identify an optimal size for each community, or at least a "maximum size" beyond which the quality and livability will decline. This approach recognizes that some communities are growing too fast and need to slow their rate of growth. Other communities may have exceeded their optimal size and need to limit additional growth.

The finite nature of our world has been all but neglected, in spite of its obvious importance. Like the Victorians who spoke of love but not of sex, many planners and policy-makers talk about reducing the impacts of growth, but not about slowing it down. An assumption is being made that we can keep on growing, if we just do it right. But no matter how you dress it up, growth is still growth. Even the best-looking, best-planned growth can still have a predominantly negative impact on a community and long-term ecological consequences. Complete reliance on planned-growth strategies is based on the false premise that you can have your cake and develop it too.

With planned, or "smart" growth, farmland and open space may disappear a little slower and urban spread may be a little less ugly, chaotic, and costly. But the bottom line is that we will continue to grow until we overburden our environment. As Colorado University Professor Albert Bartlett said, "Smart growth ultimately gets you to exactly the same place as dumb growth — you just get there first class."[11]

While good planning can mitigate many of the problems of urban growth, planned growth is not the ultimate solution. We must learn to integrate the ecological principles of sustainability into public policies for managing growth. New and innovative approaches to slowing growth are emerging. As these growth controls evolve and we gain more experience with them, communities will be empowered to truly take charge of their future.

MEET THE URBAN GROWTH MACHINE

Throughout American history the most consistent theme in local governance has been the pursuit of growth: more people, more jobs, and more real estate development. Local democracy has been dominated by "growth coalitions," composed of individuals and enterprises with a direct stake in real estate development.[1]

— Harvard economists and public policy and planning professors Alan Altshuler and Jose Gomez-Ibanez, *Regulation for Revenue*

Most cities are busily doing everything they can to grow as fast as possible. They are aggressively recruiting new businesses with subsidies, tax waivers, and other giveaways. They are pouring millions into building infrastructure to accommodate future growth. And they seem willing to sacrifice local livability and environmental quality to achieve this growth.

But who and what is behind this push to grow? Citizens who have opposed growth in their communities might feel that there is a giant conspiracy fighting against them. In fact, they're not far from the truth. There is a distinct group of well-funded and politically influential interests that tends to form a powerful pro-growth alliance. Or, as sociologist and political economist Harvey Molotch described in a classic 1976 essay, the city acts like a *growth machine*.[2]

The concept of an urban growth machine helps make sense of the various political and economic constituencies that act in their common financial interest to perpetuate growth in a typical city. An understanding of the growth machine is essential for anyone seeking to influence growth in their community.

THE NUTS AND BOLTS OF THE GROWTH MACHINE

The engine of the growth machine is powered by the fortunes resulting from land speculation and real estate development. The primary business interests are the landowners, real estate developers, mortgage bankers, realtors, construction companies and contractors, cement and sand and gravel companies, and building suppliers. While these various players may disagree on some issues, they all have a common economic interest in promoting local growth. They tend to be wealthy, organized, and politically influential in most communities.

Many of the members of these groups have organized into local and regional associations to more effectively represent their business interests: the Chamber of Commerce, Association of Realtors, Home Builders Association, and so forth. The regional associations may, in turn, be part of powerful national organizations. These business associations often have stronger pro-growth positions than the individual membership they represent.

Members of the business community tend to adopt a "growth is good" philosophy. This is based on the simplistic notion that growth will increase their business volume and they will become more prosperous. But a store owner who hopes for more customers may be forgetting that growth also brings some very tough competition. The friendly, locally owned neighborhood pharmacy may currently enjoy serving the entire west end of town. But growth is likely to bring in the big national chain stores. Local business owners are rarely a match for national firms with sophisticated marketing, volume buying power, and greater financial resources.

The small, locally owned businesses are likely to be casualties in the competition growth brings. The bigger local companies, however, are likely to do well at the top of the economic food chain. These larger businesses also tend to dominate the local chamber of commerce's pro-growth policies.

LOCAL GOVERNMENT BECOMES PART MACHINE

Pro-growth business interests recognize the important role local government has in the business of land development. Zoning codes, building permits, and other land use regulations are controlled by the local government. So, too, are investments in roads, sewers, and other public infrastructure required by development. The local government

THE ENGINE OF THE GROWTH MACHINE

Many businesses prosper with growth. Some, particularly those that dominate the market, are easy to identify. This list is headed by US West, Public Service Co., the cable TV companies, television network affiliates, King Soopers, Safeway, Albertsons, and this newspaper. The more people, the more income. It's that simple.

Another segment of this pro-growth group are those who make their living directly from growth. This group includes contractors, engineers, architects, and the biggest group of all (dollar wise), the developers ...

We have a third important pro-growth segment in Colorado — the financial institutions. Almost every developer in the state along the Front Range is in some sort of financial distress. Their distress has given the banks and savings and loans an equal amount of distress. Those financial institutions hitched their future far too tightly to the success or failure of the developers. So, like it or not, they became unambiguously pro-growth. They need to save the developers to save themselves.

So we have this major part of the Colorado business community "hooked" on growth.

— Former Colorado State Legislator Kenneth Monfort, *The Denver Post*[3]

can waive taxes on new business or industry or establish tax rates that are favorable to growth. It can create laws to protect property and maintain a police force to enforce them. It can fund economic development programs to attract new buyers and tenants for the developments.

The nature of the game is to influence the local government to improve the profitability of local land development. Local government can affect profitability by:

- increasing the intensity of land use (rezoning or annexing land, for example);

- reducing the cost of development (reducing regulations, fees, and delays);

- diverting public resources to support local land development (new roads, sewers, and other facilities); and

- stimulating the demand for new development (economic development programs, tax incentives, and other subsidies).

Molotch argues that a primary objective of the pro-growth coalition is to divert public resources into growth-inducing investments. He suggests that the local government is co-opted by these forces to such a degree that growth promotion becomes the "essence of local government."

All together these economic and political forces constitute an urban growth machine.

THE INNER WORKINGS OF THE GROWTH MACHINE

To help understand the phenomenon of the local growth machine, consider the following hypothetical scenario adapted from an article by economists Paul Huszlar and David Seckle:[4]

> A measure is placed on the ballot for a public vote. The result of approving this measure will be a cost of $100,000 and a benefit of $50,000. The costs will be distributed across 10,000 people while the benefits will be divided among only ten people. The measure creates twice as much cost as benefit, and is therefore clearly undesirable. Yet, it is likely to pass! Here's why:
>
> Each of the 10,000 people who incur a cost pay on average only $10. But the ten beneficiaries will receive an average of $5,000 each. The benefits of such a ballot measure are typically sufficient to motivate these recipients to band together, hire an attorney, and launch a publicity campaign in its favor. Even if a few beneficiaries refuse to go along, it does not matter, because the remainder have sufficient resources (net benefits after costs) to conduct the campaign.
>
> The situation is quite different for the 10,000 people incurring the cost. Since their individual loss is only $10, they will not be highly motivated to expend personal time and effort to oppose the measure. Also, since they are widely dispersed, they will have a harder time organizing and pooling resources.

Urban growth is much like this hypothetical ballot measure. The benefits flow to the few while the costs (congestion, quality of life, higher taxes) are spread among the many. Thus, according to Huszar and Seckler, "Both the distribution and the quality of benefits and costs tend to create a powerful, tightly integrated, and well-financed minority of beneficiaries opposed to a loose-knit, poorly financed majority of losers. The outcome in the political process is relative superiority of the pro-growth faction."[5]

The urban growth machine is essentially a manifestation of *The Tragedy of the Commons* as described by Garrett Hardin.[6] In this case, the "commons" is the whole community — the people, their natural environment, clean water, livability, various amenities, public facilities, tax base, and so forth. The benefits from exploiting the community

THE CLASSIC LAND DEVELOPMENT SCHEME

Making a tidy profit on land requires more than just smart buying and selling. The idea is to buy a frog and turn it into a prince. To make the big bucks, you need to do a complete "makeover" using the services of local government, compliments of local taxpayers. Here's an example of how it's done:

Step 1: Buy 200 acres of undevelopable wetlands outside the city limits for a song.

Step 2: Get the city to annex the land and rezone it for industrial use. (But it still can't be developed, due to federal wetlands protection laws.)

Step 3: Have city planning staff conduct a costly wetlands planning process (at taxpayer's expense) to enable the area's landowners to develop their land by "restoring" wetlands elsewhere.

Step 4: Get the city to declare the entire area an "enterprise zone" allowing all new businesses locating there to operate tax free for the first three to five years (directly increasing the value of this land, again at the expense of taxpayers).

Step 5: But wait, there's more! The city manager authorizes construction of $20 million in public infrastructure (sewers, roads, etc.) to serve this vacant land at no charge to the landowners.

Step 6: The local electric utility gets with the program and builds power lines and a transformer station to serve the anticipated power needs of the industrial area (compliments of the utility's rate payers).

Step 7: Feeling that they have not yet done enough, local governments fund an economic development agency to recruit big, outside corporations to the area.

Step 8: Bingo! Secret negotiations and promises of special favors, cheap labor, and expedited building permits lure a giant manufacturer to buy the land for millions of dollars. The manufacturer announces plans for a billion-dollar factory that will use millions of pounds of toxic chemicals and consume vast quantities of the community's water and electricity.

Step 9: Public concerns about the environmental, economic, and social impacts of the factory cause city staff to work overtime to expedite permit approvals and quell citizen opposition. City hires a PR firm to advise them on how to sell the development to the public.

Step 10: Factory gets built in spite of massive public opposition.

The Bottom Line: Instead of being a Ripley's "Believe it or Not," this kind of public subsidization of land development occurs in many American cities. This illustration is based on a recent case in Eugene, Oregon where the landowner made a tidy profit of a couple of million dollars at the expense of the local community, which is footing the bill for more than $50 million in subsidies that made the lucrative sale possible.

commons accrue to a few individuals (such as developers, builders, and land speculators), while the costs are distributed across the entire community. The individuals who benefit will tend to exert a strong influence to promote continued growth. They are motivated by a recognition that growth is good for them. It becomes their goal to convince others that growth is also good for the community. Oregon environmental leader Andy Kerr has called urban growth "a pyramid scheme in which a relatively few make a killing, some others make a living, but most Oregonians pay for it."[7]

The growth machine is functioning very effectively in most American cities. It tends to push citizens out of growth policy issues and is often a powerful force in funding local political campaigns and fighting citizen ballot initiatives. It works steadily to ensure that a majority of elected officials are growth-friendly. And it aggressively diverts public attention away from the negative environmental, social, and economic consequences of growth with claims that growth "makes jobs" and "provides affordable housing."

ACCESSORIES TO THE MACHINE

In addition to developers and real estate interests, there are a number of other business and professional interests who may become part of the growth machine. The local newspaper may see growth as a way to increase circulation and bring new advertisers. Each new mega-store will need to announce its entry into the local market with full page ads. The paper may also want to stay on good terms with the real estate industry due to the large volume of real estate ads most papers enjoy.

Support for the growth machine often comes from professionals whose jobs are directly connected with growth. Planners are one example. The business of planning has become primarily the process of accommodating growth. Without growth, the role of the urban planner would need to be greatly redefined. When planners are called on to evaluate growth management policies, it's not surprising that they are often less than enthusiastic about policies that might actually slow or stop growth. The fact that the planning profession depends so much on growth creates a bias away from restraining growth and toward channeling or shaping it. This may explain why so much of the professional planning literature on growth management is pessimistic about policies to moderate or stop growth. Other professionals who may find themselves part of the growth machine include architects, landscapers, engineers, surveyors, interior decorators, home inspectors, appraisers, and even wetlands consultants.

Clearly all these professionals and business owners are capable of acting in the broader public interest — even when it might adversely impact their own interests. This description is not intended to impugn the character or integrity of any of the participants in the growth machine. The concept of a growth machine merely creates an awareness of the system of financial incentives that have kept us on the path of growth.

Some people may feel that the concept of a growth machine also applies to the interests of big businesses around the world. This may be true, but the urban growth machine is a uniquely local phenomenon. It may be strong and powerful in some cities and weak, or non-existent, in others. It functions primarily at the local level, but often forms coalitions to influence statewide policies.

USING DEMOCRACY TO CONTROL THE GROWTH MACHINE

A good local government can play a major role in developing responsible growth policies. Unfortunately, many local governments are thoroughly entwined with the narrow, special interests of the growth machine. The control of local government by special interests is, of course, inconsistent with the principles of democracy. The solution is better government. As H.L. Mencken once said, "The cure for the [ills] of democracy is more democracy."

While this book is not about how to create good government or how to run political campaigns, there are a few general principles that can be applied here. Good government should be dedicated to serving the broader public interests of the community it serves. It should be open, accountable and accessible to all citizens. It should seek to keep its citizens informed and actively involve them in public policy development. It should provide accurate, complete, and balanced information to policy-makers and the public. And it should embrace the principle of "government of the people, by the people and for the people."

Here are some ways to get more democracy, resulting in better government:

- **Actively encourage public participation.** Good governments should acknowledge the value of citizen participation and cultivate it. Strong citizen involvement almost always produces a better product, whether it's a proposed development or a new public policy. It may take some effort to get citizens interested, informed, and engaged in an issue. Simply running an ad in the paper announcing a public hearing may not be enough.

- **Restore citizen balance to public land use policy-making.** In many communities the concept of balance has been distorted to such a degree that local land use "Citizen Advisory Committees" are composed almost entirely of so-called "stakeholders" — people with a direct financial interest in the outcome. City officials will appoint a 12-member committee with ten representatives from all aspects of the development industry. The two remaining slots will be given to a representative of the League of Women Voters, for example, and an "at large" citizen. A more representative citizen advisory committee would be composed entirely of volunteers from the community who are all financially detached from the outcome of an issue. The committee can invite vested interests, or stake-holders, to participate in a non-voting capacity.

- **Get the money out of politics.** It's hard to find an easier cause to support than campaign finance reform. Placing limits on the size of political contributions and requiring full disclosure of contributors is basic to restoring democracy to local politics. Communities can go further to enhance the principles of democratic governance with a good voter's pamphlet, partial public funding of politi-cal campaigns, and proportional representation in elected offices.

- **Form a grassroots organization.** An organized presence to represent the general public interest in growth and land development issues can be very effective. Form a group like Citizens for the Future, Friends of Our Town, or Coalition for Responsible Land Use. Organizational details are not especially important, but the more members, and the bigger the mailing list, the better. The next time the newspaper needs to get a "contrasting opinion" on a proposed local development, they'll know where to go.

- **Hire a *public advocate* for land use and planning.** A pub-lic advocate (PA) can be hired by the local government to represent the public's interest in major land use decision-making processes.[8] The PA helps to balance a process that is typically dominated by the developer's attorney and other hired consultants. Unlike most citizens, the PA can devote full time to public interest representation. The PA might be an attorney or professional planner who can bring a high level of expertise before the local council or planning commission. The PA can file testimony and present witnesses and other experts to develop a more complete record for a case. The PA can also serve as an information resource for citizens concerned about a development proposal.

Additional tools required to control the growth machine can be found in the following chapters of this book. These chapters are intended to provide the reader with a clear understanding of the key growth issues that shape public policy. When growth issues are given a more balanced treatment, and a greater public awareness of growth impacts is achieved, the broader public interest has a better chance of prevailing. With the right growth controls and a vision for the future, the growth machine will no longer dominate local growth policies.

THE TWELVE BIG MYTHS OF GROWTH

Growth for the sake of growth is the ideology of the cancer cell.

— Edward Abbey

The issue of urban growth is permeated with stereotyping, platitudes, clichés, rhetoric, questionable assumptions, and outright myths. If you are involved in local growth issues you will encounter many statements about the necessity and benefits of continued growth. Statements such as "we have to grow or die," or "we have to grow to get new tax revenue," are repeatedly made to justify growth. They are often proffered as conventional wisdom and usually made in an unqualified manner with no supporting evidence.

The same rhetoric is repeated at public hearings, neighborhood meetings, town halls, and city council meetings across the country. The community is urged to make concessions and sacrifices for development in order to gain alleged benefits such as new jobs, a bigger tax base, or some vague promise of economic prosperity. We are told that slowing growth would be disastrous and that even if we wanted to slow growth, it would be impossible.

But where is the careful analysis that gives people the confidence to make such claims? When such rhetoric is accepted and not questioned, it results in many poor public policies that fail to serve the greater public welfare. It is important to get beyond the rhetoric in order to base local discussion and decision-making on more substantive and objective information. Only then can we start to have

TEST YOUR KNOWLEDGE ABOUT GROWING CITIES:

1. The bigger cities get, the lower local taxes are. T or F?
2. The faster cities grow, the lower local taxes are. T or F?
3. Police protection costs (per capita) are less in bigger cities. T or F?
4. Crime rates are higher in bigger cities. T or F?
5. The more cities grow, the more people are unemployed. T or F?
6. Bigger cities tend to have a lower cost of living and housing. T or F?
7. Growth creates costs, but the new tax revenues more than offset the added expenses. T or F?
8. More business subsidies mean greater prosperity for local residents. T or F?
9. Environmental regulation is bad for the economy. T or F?
10. Developed land usually produces more net revenues for the city (tax revenues minus cost of public services) than undeveloped land. T or F?

[Answers: 1) F; 2) F; 3) F; 4) T; 5) T; 6) F; 7) F; 8) F; 9) F; 10) F.]

meaningful discourse resulting in balanced and informed views about growth and its impacts.

The solution to all the rhetoric is simple: better information. This chapter challenges what has essentially become the mythology surrounding urban growth (see Figure 3-1). It may encourage you to ask new questions and seek answers based on credible data and analysis, not conjecture and wishful thinking. Most local governments are capable of providing the balanced, quality information citizens need to make informed decisions about growth — you just have to ask for it!

DEBUNKING THE MYTHOLOGY

The four biggest growth myths are about taxes, jobs, economic prosperity, and housing. Because these are complex and fundamental issues, they are given more attention in the next two chapters. Chapter 4 explores the relationships between jobs, housing and growth. Chapter 5 examines the real costs of growth and how they impact local taxpayers.

Myth I: Growth provides needed tax revenues.

Reality Check: Growth tends to *raise* local tax rates. The direct and indirect costs of urban growth place new demands on local resources and

Figure 3-1
The Common Growth Mythology

Myth 1: Growth provides needed tax revenues.

Myth 2: We have to grow to provide jobs for people in the community.

Myth 3: We must stimulate and subsidize business growth to have good jobs.

Myth 4: If we try to limit growth, housing prices will shoot up.

Myth 5: Environmental protection hurts the economy. We must be willing to sacrifice local environmental quality for jobs and economic prosperity.

Myth 6: Growth is inevitable. Growth management doesn't work and therefore we have no choice but to continue growing. You can't put a fence around our town.

Myth 7: If you don't like growth, you're a "NIMBY"(not in my back yard) or an "ANTI" (against everything).

Myth 8: Most people don't really support growth management or environmental protection.

Myth 9: We have to "grow or die." Growth makes the economy strong and creates better-paying jobs.

Myth 10: Vacant or undeveloped land is just going to waste.

Myth 11: A person's visual preference is no basis for objecting to development.

Myth 12: Environmentalists are just another special interest. There is no such thing as the public interest.

divert money away from other important public services.

We hear that the more people and businesses we attract to our community, the more tax revenues we will have. Supposedly this will generate surplus funds and enable us to get more public services or pay for a new library or concert hall we couldn't have afforded otherwise, without increasing our individual tax burden. Citizens hoping for a tax windfall from new development are likely to be disappointed. While growth does result in a larger overall tax base, it usually costs more money than it generates, resulting in a net fiscal drain. Harvard economists Alan Altshuler and Jose Gomez-Ibanez report that:

> "The available evidence shows that development does not cover new public cost; that is, it brings in less revenue for local governments than the price of servicing it." [1]

In spite of the available evidence, there is an astonishing lack of awareness about the relationship between urban growth and local taxes. One possible reason is the number of good studies looking at this relationship is still quite small. While our local governments spend billions of dollars every year on new infrastructure to serve growth, few have deemed it worthwhile to examine how much it costs, who pays for it and who benefits from it.

The first piece of the picture is that larger cities tend to have higher per capita taxes.[2] The bigger the city, the higher the taxes. According to the empirical data, it is unlikely that becoming a larger city will reduce our tax burden. How, then, have so many people come to believe that growth will bring some sort of tax relief?

The relationship between urban growth and local taxes was investigated in two separate studies in Illinois. Both used statistical methods to examine the relationship between growth and increasing property taxes. Local governments in Illinois depend heavily on property taxes, as do most cities and counties in the U.S.

The first study was done in 1991 by the DuPage County Planning Department.[3] DuPage County Planning Director Delip Bammi noticed that as the county grew, taxes kept going up, rather than down as they were supposed to. This was especially surprising, considering the county had been growing rapidly for the past 20 years and had received more than its share of regional job growth, business expansion, and commercial development. Bammi commissioned a study to see if there was a relationship between growth and taxes. This study found two strong correlations: new development tended to *increase* property taxes; and communities in the county with the most rapid growth tended to have the greatest tax increases.

His findings were so noteworthy that they made the cover of *The Wall Street Journal*. According to Bammi, he received many calls from other planning directors across the county who said they had also noticed that growth appeared to cause higher taxes in their counties. They would then ask him how he had managed to keep his job after publishing such a report. It's an ugly tribute to the power of the urban growth machine that many planners and public officials find their job is on the line when they try to provide basic public information on growth impacts.

The second, broader study by the Metropolitan Planning Council (greater Chicago area) in 1995 looked at the six-county region surrounding Chicago.[4] This study confirmed the earlier findings in DuPage County and reached several more general conclusions: population growth tends to increase the residential tax burden (measured as a percent of personal income); and fast-growing areas that do not increase taxes will tend to see a reduction in public services. These findings fly in the face of everything we typically hear about the alleged tax benefits of growth.

While the findings summarized above tell us that the overall fiscal impacts of growth may be negative, they don't tell us why these effects occur. The simplest explanation for why growth places a net burden on local resources is that it creates a need for costly new infrastructure to serve new development — roads, sewers, water treatment capacity, new schools, libraries, police stations, parks, etc. While the taxes paid by new development are generally designed to cover the cost of providing ongoing public services, they are not adequate to cover the additional capital costs of the new and expanded facilities the development requires. A new house, for example, can cost local taxpayers $20,000 to $30,000 or more for the new public facilities required to serve it. (For a better understanding of why growth doesn't pay its own way, see Chapter 5: Discovering the Real Cost of Growth in Your Community.)

The bottom line on urban growth is that it rarely pays its own way. This is a powerful argument for new growth controls. Whenever a development proponent claims that a tax windfall will be generated by a new project, the burden of proof should be on the development proponent, not the community. It is far more prudent to assume new development will be a net drain rather than a net gain to the local treasury. Chapter 5 describes how a *fiscal impact analysis*, and other types of analyses, can be used to resolve this question for a major development proposal in your community. Other types of development impact statements, such as community impact statements, are described in Chapter 6 and can provide a broader range of information about a prospective development.

Myth 2: We have to grow to provide jobs for people in the community.

Reality Check: We can't grow our way out of local unemployment problems. Growth just makes the problem bigger.

The overly simplistic logic goes like this: Everybody agrees that people need jobs, therefore, anything that creates jobs must be good. If you oppose growth, then "you don't care about people who need jobs." According to University of California, Santa Barbara Professor Harvey Molotch, "A key ideological prop for the growth machine, especially in appealing to the working class, is the assertion that local growth 'makes jobs.' This claim is aggressively promulgated by developers, bankers, and Chamber of Commerce officials."[5]

The real question is not whether growth creates jobs, but whether it reduces local unemployment. Presumably, if growth reduced unemployment, a fast-growing city would tend to have a lower unemployment rate than a slow-growing one. To test this, Molotch examined two decades of census data on growth rates and unemployment.[6] He compared unemployment rates in the 25 fastest growing cities in the U.S. with the 25 slowest growing. He found no statistical correlation between the growth rate and the unemployment rate. Faster-growing cities are undoubtedly creating new jobs, but, it seems they are also attracting new residents who don't find jobs. The faster-growing city ends up being a bigger city, with a similar unemployment rate and a larger number of people unemployed.

> **THE JOB CREATION PARADOX: CREATING JOBS INCREASES THE NUMBER OF PEOPLE OUT OF WORK**
>
> When people are free to move from one community (town, city, county, state) to another, job creation in a community will cause people from outside to move in to take the jobs. As a consequence, the population of the community will grow sufficiently to restore the equilibrium unemployment rate of four percent to six percent. By the time sufficient jobs have been created to double the size of the community, the number of people out of work will have doubled.
>
> Community leaders want people to believe that their efforts to create jobs are motivated by altruism. In fact, job creation is a mechanism for promoting population growth in the community.
>
> If a community wishes to create jobs and then maintain itself as an island of low unemployment, it must erect barriers to prevent the in-migration of unemployed people.[7]
>
> — Dr. Albert Bartlett, Universiy of Colorado.

Economic booms may provide temporary relief from unemployment woes, but experience clearly indicates that growth is not the long-term solution to unemployment. Creating more local jobs ends up attracting more people, who require more jobs, as explained by Albert Bartlett in the *Job Creation Paradox*.

Myth 3: We must stimulate and subsidize business growth to have good jobs.

Reality Check: Traditional economic development programs are often little more than corporate subsidies that act to fuel local growth. Taxpayer money is wasted and few public benefits can be shown.

This is a variation on Myth 2 that emphasizes business growth. The reasoning goes like this: People want good jobs; jobs come from businesses; therefore, creating a good business climate will result in more good jobs. A "good business climate" roughly translates to one with less government regulation, lower taxes, and a higher level of business subsidies.

A study by Dr. William R. Freudenburg of the University of Wisconsin evaluated how well business-climate ratings predict the prosperity of the people living in those areas.[8] He used the three best known business climate ratings (*Inc. Magazine*, the U.S. Chamber of Commerce, and the Fantus Company) and compared the performance of each state, five and ten years after its rating. States with "good" business climate ratings actually had *worse* economic outcomes than the states with "bad" business climates. People in the states with the worst business climate ratings experienced $585 to $1,100 *more* growth in per capita income after five years than did top-ranked states. The disparity was even greater after ten years.

The study did not address short-term gains. However, over the long run, an individual can expect to receive higher personal income gains in states rated as having bad business climates. This surprising outcome may be due to the emphasis placed by good-business-climate states on investing resources in businesses rather than directly in people. Chapter 4 takes a closer look at some of the inherent problems with traditional economic development programs and the alternatives for improving local prosperity.

Myth 4: If we try to limit growth, housing prices will shoot up.

Reality Check: Growth controls can produce many benefits for a community and may even result in a better distribution of affordable housing than market-driven growth.

Housing affordability has the potential to become a key issue in any local debate about how to control growth. The development industry has repeatedly used the housing affordability issue to defeat growth controls on the grounds that anything that restricts the supply of housing, or pushes up the cost, will affect housing affordability.

Concerns about how growth controls affect the availability of low and moderate-income housing are legitimate. But such concerns should not be used merely to thwart and undermine growth controls.

Rather, these concerns should serve as the motivation to create responsible policies that truly address the community's housing needs.

A 1992 study compared housing prices of seven California cities having growth controls with comparable cities not having growth controls.[9] This study examined each community's home prices every year from 1980 to 1987 and found that "median single-family home prices did not rise any faster or to higher levels in the seven case-study cities than in their counterpart pro-growth cities. Indeed, by the end of the 1980s, housing was more affordable in some of the growth control cities than in their corresponding comparison cities." The report concludes that, "Home prices need not be systematically higher or increase faster in growth control cities than in pro-growth cities."

One explanation for why housing prices would be lower in cities with growth controls is that cities acting to control growth may also be more proactive with housing policies. Indeed, an extensive survey of California's 443 cities and counties found that municipalities with growth controls enacted more affordable housing incentives than cities without growth controls.[10]

Portland, Oregon went from being called the "most livable city" in the nation to "the second least affordable" within a few years. What happened? The local Home Builders Association blamed Portland's urban growth boundary for restricting the supply of cheap land. They argued that, if the boundary were expanded, there would be more land available at lower cost for new residential subdivisions. They say that these savings will be passed on to new home buyers, thereby helping to solve the affordability problem.

While it seems logical that the cost of land contributes to the cost of new housing, there are many other factors influencing housing affordability. For example, land prices are rising faster in many cities without growth boundaries than they are in Portland. From 1990 to 1995 median lot prices rose faster in Oklahoma City, Charlotte North Carolina, Chattanooga Tennessee, Salt Lake City, and Houston than they did in Portland.[11]

Both the supply and demand for housing affect price. In most cases, it is rapid growth pressures that drive up prices. These growth pressures are usually the result of an expanding economy that is creating jobs and attracting new residents. Portland's higher housing prices are primarily a reflection of a sharp increase in the demand to live in there. Portland has always been a desirable place to live with an attractive natural environment but, until recently, there have been few jobs for newcomers and existing residents had to settle for less-than-average salaries. The city's urban growth boundary has been in place for more than 18 years. But housing prices did not start to climb until the local economy picked up in 1989.

Housing affordability is defined in terms of what the local median household income can afford. Thus, the affordability issue is largely one of local income levels. The nationwide shift from higher paying manufacturing jobs to lower paying retail and service sector jobs has contributed to the problem. The wage rates offered by new local jobs strongly influence housing affordability.

Whether or not the community has growth controls in place may not be the deciding factor when it comes to how growth pressures affect housing prices. Instead, the rate of growth, the kinds of new jobs being created, and the kinds of housing policies enacted are likely to be more important influences.

As with the *job creation paradox* (see Myth 2), local solutions to housing problems suffer from the lack of boundaries. It is difficult to provide housing for those in your community who need it, when the demand for affordable housing is nationwide and people are free to move in and consume whatever lower-cost housing the community has provided. This difficulty is addressed in the next chapter.

If housing affordability is indeed the problem faced by a community, then what is the best solution? Unfettered sprawl without growth limits might lower housing costs slightly for awhile. But abandoning growth controls will not solve housing affordability problems, and unrestricted growth is likely to create even more problems. Chapter 4 offers solutions to housing needs that can save taxpayers money and do not involve sacrificing the local environment or compromising quality of life.

Myth 5: Environmental protection hurts the economy. We must be willing to sacrifice local environmental quality for jobs and economic prosperity.

Reality check: Environmental protection is good for people and the economy.

A 1993 comparison of environmental standards and economic growth by Bank of America Vice President and Senior Economist Frederick Cannon, found that the economies of states with strong environmental standards had grown nearly one-half a percent faster per year during the previous 14 years than in states with weak environmental standards.[12]

Massachusetts Institute of Technology professor Stephen Meyer posed the question: Does environmental protection and regulation hinder economic growth, job creation, and overall production, as some business groups maintain?[13] He evaluated and ranked the 50 states based on two sets of criteria: economic prosperity (gross domestic product, total employment, and productivity); and breadth and depth of environmental programs. Meyers found that:

- states with stronger environmental policies consistently out-performed the weaker environmental states on all economic measures;

- the pursuit of environmental quality does not hinder economic growth and development;

- there appears to be a moderate, yet consistent, positive association between environmentalism and economic growth; and

- there is no evidence that relaxing environmental standards will produce economic growth.

A similar study by the Institute for Southern Studies (1994) ranked the 50 states in two categories: Environmental Health (green index) and Economic Health (gold index).[14] Twenty indicators were used in

Figure 3-2
Top and Bottom rankings for Combined Economic Health(Gold)
and Environmental Health (Green)

Top 10 States		Gold Rank	Green Rank	Bottom 10 States		Gold Rank	Green Rank
1	Vermont	3	1	41	Arkansas	47	37
2	Hawaii	1	4	42	Indiana	38	47
3	New Hampshire	6	2	43	Kentucky	45	40
4	Minnesota	2	7	44	South Carolina	44	42
5	Wisconsin	9	6	45	Tennessee	41	48
6	Colorado	11	5	46	Texas	40	49
7	Oregon	8	9	47	Alabama	46	46
8	Massachusetts	12	8	48	Mississippi	49	43
9	Connecticut	4	18	49	West Virginia	48	45
10	Maryland	10	12	50	Louisiana	50	50

Source: Institute for Southern Studies, 1994.

each category to create the rankings. Nine of the states ranked among the top 12 on the environmental scale also ranked among the top 12 on the economic scale. Conversely, 12 states ranked among the 14 worst on both lists. This study supports the conclusion that environmental protection and economic prosperity go hand-in-hand. According to the report, "The states that do the most to protect their natural resources also wind up with the strongest economies and the best jobs for their citizens."

A study published by the American Chemical Society found that states with lower pollution levels (based on chemical emissions per job) have stronger economies as reflected in lower unemployment rates.[15] They also have better environmental quality and lower energy use.

Myth 6: Growth is inevitable. Growth management doesn't work and therefore we have no choice but to continue growing. You can't put a fence around our town.

Reality Check: You can establish limits to growth and you can create a "railing" around your community.

Because it is impractical and also illegal to build a physical barrier to the movement of people and goods within the U.S., growth advocates suggest that there is nothing productive you can do to keep your community at the size you like.

The statement that "growth is inevitable" implies that we are helpless victims of change, that we must accept whatever growth is thrust upon us, and that our only choice is the manner in which we accommodate it.

It is true that our communities cannot erect tall fences, build insurmountable walls, or use drawbridges over alligator-filled moats to keep people out. There is a constitutional *right to travel* that prevents communities from erecting these kinds of rigid barriers. But that doesn't mean there is nothing we can do to rein in growth. We can use a wide range of responsible policies and regulations to influence whether or not people and businesses choose to locate in our community. We can also set limits to the rate of growth and even cap the ultimate size of our community.

One option is to adopt policies that will discourage undesirable kinds of growth. By enacting specific standards, a community can create what might be termed a "railing." This railing, unlike the proverbial fence, might be composed of environmental, social, and economic standards that will direct growth and change in the community without blocking it entirely. (For more on growth standards, see Chapter 6: Putting the Brakes on Growth — What Works?)

Dozens of communities have established limits to their rate of growth and to their ultimate size to protect the local quality of life and to respect the physical limitations of their natural environment. These growth limits have yet to be thoroughly tested in the courts. But the ability to establish limits seems like a reasonable, if not essential, tool for community governance. The idea of unlimited, or forced, growth is repulsive. It implies a horrible sickness, like a cancer.

Some growth limits will cap the ultimate population size of a community. This must be done in a manner that does not prevent people from coming and going. While the size of the population may be stabilized, the composition can remain dynamic within the bounds set by the community. As long as new births and in-migration do not exceed deaths and out-migration, the community does not grow.

As more and more communities realize they want to preserve their small town character, the idea of establishing limits to growth will become more commonplace. As some communities reach the limits they have set for themselves and stop growing, the courts — and society — will make decisions about how this transition to a stable community may properly occur.

Myth 7: If you don't like growth, you're a "NIMBY" or an "Anti."

Reality Check: NIMBYs have valid concerns.

The overused NIMBY acronym, "not in my back yard," is supposed to reflect a selfish attitude, an unwillingness to accept some undesirable development in, or near, the neighborhood. Similar rhetorical labels include "anti's" (people who are against everything), "gatekeepers", "drawbridge raisers", or "I've got mine." There are far too many examples of how these negative labels have been used against concerned citizens to neutralize opposition to growth.

These labels seem to have the primary purpose of invalidating what may be very legitimate concerns about growth and development. A NIMBY is more likely to be someone who cares enough about the future of his or her community to get out and protect it. You can thank all the great NIMBYs of the past for keeping hazardous wastes dumps, major polluters, and other nuisances out of your community. The more people join together to preserve the quality of their "backyards," the better off the world will be.

People who move to a community and then express concerns about growth are sometimes referred to as "pulling up the drawbridge after them." Again, this is likely to be a distortion of the person's real motives. Often, newcomers to a community move there because they recognize it has some special qualities. They may also have lived in other towns where they've watched similar qualities be destroyed by growth. Thus, they may have a keen awareness of how vulnerable their new community's assets are. This outside experience can be valuable to a community that has not recently experienced the consequences of rapid growth.

People who want slow growth tend to be those who care very much about the future of their community and want to protect what they value for generations to come. They are usually volunteers who are willing to contribute their time generously in a charitable civic capacity to improve the community and the environment. Is it more accurate for the local newspaper to refer to such a person as *anti-growth* or as *pro-community*? Negative labeling distorts and marginalizes legitimate viewpoints. It also tends to polarize issues and discourage productive dialogue. Are you an *anti-growther* or a *dedicated civic volunteer* concerned about the future of your community?

Myth 8: Most don't really support growth management or environmental protection.

Reality Check: A majority of the public does recognize the importance of environmental protection and the need to manage growth.

Surveys consistently show a broad awareness of environmental issues and a concern about continued growth. A statewide survey of 1,361 Oregonians conducted in 1993 found 75 percent of respondents believe maintaining a quality environment is more important to economic growth than relaxing environmental regulations.[16] Furthermore, 64 percent felt that "environmental protection will become more important than economic growth."

Nationwide, 70 percent of respondents to a May 1995 ABC/ *Washington Post* poll thought the federal government had not gone far enough to protect the environment. *Money* magazine found that its readers rated clean air and water above all other factors (even a low crime rate) in deciding where to live, according to its September 1995 survey.

Despite growth often being portrayed as a divisive issue with two opposed "camps," it really should not be. In areas that have experi-

CASE STUDY: NAME-CALLING IN COBURG HILLS, OREGON
(or How to Win Friends and Influence People)

The rural community of Country View Estates consists of about 25 homes on five-acre lots nestled in the scenic Coburg Hills several miles north of Eugene, Oregon. The community is surrounded by forest land. Under the existing zoning for the area, no new residential lots could be created and only a few more houses could be added.

A developer bought 150 acres of forest land next to the community. The property was a mixture of farm and forest land and already had a house on it. The forest zoning allowed him to build only one additional house for the purpose of managing his timber lands. But he saw greater profits if he could rezone the land, subdivide the property, and sell off five-, ten-, or 20-acre homesites.

The neighbors objected to the rezoning application for many reasons. The development would partially destroy the undeveloped forested setting they had built their homes in. It would also put their water supply at risk, increase traffic, and permanently affect the character of the area.

The neighbors filed a formal opposition to the rezoning and defeated it. However, in a local newspaper article, and later at the public hearing, the developer's agent rudely insulted the neighbors, saying they were "selfish," and they just didn't "want anyone else coming in and obstructing their views." While these statements were completely irrelevant to the rezoning decision, they hit their intended mark.

The next year the same developer tried again to rezone his land. This time the neighbors did not object. The rezoning was approved, even though it could have been defeated again. This sort of labeling and name-calling has been used effectively by countless developers to neutralize opposition to their projects.

enced rapid growth, public opinion surveys consistently show that a strong majority of the public will support policies to curb growth. A 1988 survey of Los Angeles residents found that 75 percent favored slowing or stopping growth (59 percent slowing, 16 percent stopping).[17]

A 1995 statewide survey in Colorado asked: "In general, what do you consider to be the one most important issue facing Colorado today?"[18] Respondents were not prompted to give any particular answer. "Too much growth" was the most common response, and was given more than twice as frequently as the next most common reply. The following are the top four of 15 categories of responses:

Growth, too much/too fast	34%
Crime/Drugs/Alcohol	16%
Environment	8%
Economic Problems	6%

Another question in this survey asked: "How do you feel about the overall rate of population growth in the state of Colorado. Would you say that in the past two or three years the population of the state has grown too fast, at about the right rate, or would you say that Colorado is not growing fast enough?" The responses were:

Too fast	73%
About right	24%
Not fast enough	1%
Don't know	2%

Myth 9: We have to "grow or die." Growth makes the economy strong and creates better paying jobs.

Reality Check: The short-term benefits of additional growth may not outweigh the longer-term costs.

According to ecological economist Herman Daly, "There is evidence that in the United States growth now makes us poorer by increasing costs faster than it increases benefits. In other words, we appear to have grown beyond the optimal scale."[19]

Daly and others have shown that the growing U.S. gross domestic product (GDP) does not reflect the true economic welfare of the public. While GDP has grown steadily, better measures of economic welfare that consider social and ecological costs, such as the Genuine Progress Indicator, show a declining level of prosperity over the past 20 years (see Figure 3-3).

While acknowledging the political difficulty in limiting growth, Daly has argued convincingly that we must move towards a stable or "steady-state" economy. While a stable economy can continue to develop in a qualitative sense, quantitative growth in material consumption and waste production cannot continue indefinitely.

The idea that economies must grow seems to be rooted in classical economics originating more than 200 years ago. These early economists believed that population growth was inevitable (there were no safe and effective birth control devices at the time). Thus, they believed economies must grow to meet the needs of expanding populations. However, in recent times, many European countries have shown that they can have strong, prosperous economies with little or no population growth.

The bias toward continued growth in gross economic output is apparent in the professional terminology. A non-growing economy is referred to as "stagnant" or even "recessionary," rather than the more accurate and neutral term, stable. The former terms imply rot, decay, and decline, while the later implies balance and equilibrium.

North American society has very little experience with economies that are *intentionally* stable or non-growing in terms of consumption and pollution emission. The business of crafting a sustainable economy that does not place increasing burdens on the natural environment will be a challenge for the future. Chapter 7 looks at the prospects for sustainable communities and economies.

Figure 3-3
Gross Domestic Product
Compared with Genuine Progress Indicator[20]

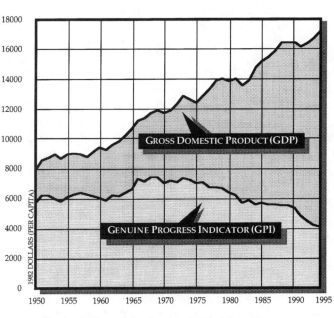

Reprinted with permission. Copyright 1995, Redefining Progress.

FEAR OF DYING IN EUGENE, OREGON

In 1995, various members of Eugene's business community were trying to promote a proposal for a new convention center that would cost at least $25 million and require ongoing public subsidies. The vice president of marketing for the Hilton Hotel (the largest local hotel) was quoted in the newspaper as saying "We have to grow or die." The statement went unchallenged by the reporter in spite of the fact that the hotel had been profitable for the past 20 years without any growth.

Myth 10: Vacant or undeveloped land is just going to waste.

Reality Check: Open space and farmland are valuable and irreplaceable assets that contribute significantly to every community.

An undeveloped or idle piece of land is viewed by some as wasteful and unproductive. Virtually any other use is better than leaving it undeveloped, they feel. In part, this perception also implies that the land, like a lazy loafer, is placing a net drain on the community that could be rectified if it were just developed.

The low assessment of the benefits of undeveloped land rests on a number of questionable assumptions. The first is that undeveloped land is a burden on the community. Actually, undeveloped land requires few, if any, public services and there is little or no public cost required to maintain it. Studies by the American Farmland Trust (AFT) consistently show that farmland and open space pay more in taxes than they require in services, providing a net surplus to the community. "Cows don't go to school," they like to point out.

The AFT's latest "Cost of Community Services Study" was performed in Frederick County, Maryland.[21] They found that farmland and open space required only $.53 in services for every dollar paid in taxes, creating a surplus and helping to make up for the budget shortfall created by residential land. Residential land required $1.14 for every dollar paid, resulting in a $20 million net loss to the county in 1995. A similar study of four New Hampshire towns conducted in 1995 found that each had a net revenue gain from open space and a net loss for residential land.[22]

Chapter 6 describes various methods for protecting farmland and open space. Case studies reported in that chapter show that in many places it will be cheaper for a community to purchase undeveloped land rather than to allow it to be developed and paying the increased costs of providing infrastructure and services.

The second questionable assumption is that this undeveloped land is producing nothing. At a minimum, the land is likely to be contributing property taxes to the community. But the land is quietly creating a whole set of benefits for the community, including peace and quiet. Valuing open space in an economic sense can be difficult, but not impossible. A greenway in Boulder, Colorado increased property values by $5.4 million and resulted in an $500,000 increase in annual property tax revenues according to a 1978 study.[23]

We have all felt the pang of regret at the loss of a particular area of open space in our community. What was that land contributing to our life that will cause us to miss it — a relaxing view, a sense of comforting tranquility, an oasis of nature, a refuge from urban constructs, a buffer from noisy roads and factories? Perhaps we are also disturbed by the permanence of the loss. The farmer's pasture that has sprouted an outlet mall will never again graze sheep.

The third questionable assumption is that the land would generate more overall benefits for the community if it were developed. There are certainly cases where this is true, but many more where it is not. If a house is built, the land is said to be "productive" because it is providing shelter for a family. But this logic assumes that if the land were undeveloped, the family would be sleeping out under the stars. The reality is that the family who would have bought or rented the house, will simply buy or rent somewhere else. The homeless person's plight will not be resolved either way.

Undeveloped land has another value which is similar to having a savings account that you never use. You don't have to spend it to appreciate that it's there in the event you need it. Communities without adequate open space or vacant land have spent their savings accounts and have limited their options for the future.

Myth 11: A person's visual preference is no basis for objecting to development.

Reality Check: The beauty of land is priceless and its destruction is permanent.

Citizens who oppose a development because it will ruin a pleasing view, or an attractive natural setting are often trivialized and dismissed by local officials who feel that profits and economic criteria are what is important. However, a pleasing natural view can be one of the most significant qualities in a good community. Unfortunately many people tend to dismiss such benefits of natural landscapes. It's all too rare that human development is a visual improvement upon a natural setting.

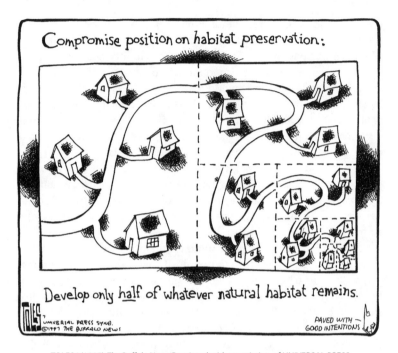

Compromise position on habitat preservation:

Develop only h<u>a</u>lf of whatever natural habitat remains.

PAVED WITH —
GOOD INTENTIONS

Seldom is a development stopped because it will harm an attractive natural setting. However, the "view" is often the most important siting criteria for a home or commercial development. The right "view" can make a $100,000 home sell for twice as much.

A 1994 study by the National Association of Home Builders found that the surrounding environment is the single most important factor affecting the market value of a home.[24] A mountain vista or the proximity to a park, beach, or stream affects home value more than the size of the house (square footage), number of rooms, pools, or appliances. When visual preferences carry such a price tag, they can hardly be dismissed as trivial.

The aesthetic values of undeveloped land probably represent other human values as well. Our preference for natural landscapes may reflect an innate appreciation for the multitude of ecological values that can be derived from them — clean air and water, wildlife habitat, species diversity, etc.— as well as the food-generating potential from hunting and foraging that our ancestors depended on. The quality of our surrounding environment is still a direct reflection of our own health and well-being. Urban natural areas can also be extremely significant to children as places to play, explore, and build a closer relationship with nature.

Myth 12: Environmentalists are just another special interest. There is no such thing as the public interest.

Reality Check: Environmentalism is both a general interest and a public interest.

It seems that the idea of a *public interest* has fallen on hard times. Nobody can put their finger on a precise definition of the concept. As a result, environmentalists (and civic activists) tend to be labeled as just another special interest. This labeling marginalizes the environmentalists' viewpoint and makes it seem that they are no different than special interest business groups. For example, a city council might appoint two chemical company representatives and two environmentalists to a committee and assume that these "special interests" would balance out to represent the "public interest."

In another variation on this theme, the city council appoints a citizen involvement committee (CIC) composed of stakeholders. The stakeholders are selected to represent every business group that might be financially impacted by the decision under consideration. In this case, CIC should stand for *Conflict of Interest Committee*. The public interest is rarely served by such appointments.

Business groups typically represents the narrow, private, profit-making interests of a relatively small segment of the community. The focus of such groups is on maximizing short-term economic gain for their particular industry, and they are undoubtedly a special interest in the political sense. Other issues are only important as they relate to this focus. The person who represents a business group on a civic committee is usually financially compensated for representing the group and may receive direct business benefits from committee participation, such as policies and decisions favorable to his or her business.

On the other hand, an environmentalist typically represents a broad range of interests and multiple values that are oriented toward protecting the current and future quality of our environmental support system. The outcome of the environmentalist's interest is the long-term welfare of all citizens and the natural habitat we ultimately depend upon. There is rarely any personal financial reward associated with the environmentalist's positions and more often, this representation

ACTION ITEM:
FORM A LOCAL TRUTH SQUAD

Ask the local media not to print clichés and puffy rhetoric. Insist that alleged benefits of growth be substantiated and that costs be considered as well as revenues. Provide local officials and media with your own documentation of growth impacts using some of the sources referenced in this and subsequent chapters. Ask your local government to help resolve questions about the impacts of growth and development proposals by providing useful data and analyses.

comes at a personal cost.

In spite of making the above distinctions between a special interest and a general interest, it is important to recognize that everyone has their own set of values and biases. Is it really possible to identify such a thing as the public interest? John Rawls, in his book *A Theory of Justice*, describes a powerful tool for exploring a state of bias-free decision-making. He calls it the "Veil of Ignorance." We can imagine this veil descending around us. When the veil is lifted we will find ourselves transported to an unknown time and place in the present, near future, or distant future. Our identity, nationality, race, age, wealth, and appearance are all unknown to us until the veil is lifted. We will exist in this new time and place for the rest of our lives.

From behind the veil of ignorance we are able to see that there is, in fact, a bias-free state from which we can judge our actions today. This exercise makes it clear that if we were sent into the future, we would not want the people of the present consuming all of the natural resources that we might also want. Nor would we want them to leave us with scarred landscapes or environmental messes they were too lazy to clean up. From behind the veil, we can see that there may be a clear and universal notion of the public interest in connection with many issues.

The *public interest* can also be defined within the context of *sustainability*. As with the Veil of Ignorance, the practice of protecting the viability of future generations requires that we consider their likely needs and avoid pre-empting their alternative paths to survival.

On any given subject, the public interest of your community must be defined by a public process. The key issue is not really what the public interest is, but how to structure a fair, open, and representative public process for determining what the community really wants and needs. The concept of democracy is one of *governing in the public interest*. But our system of representative democracy has many limitations and needs to be continually bolstered by local public involvement processes. We can start by making sure that citizen involvement committees are composed entirely of citizens who don't have any direct financial conflict of interest in the decision at hand.

MORE MYTHOLOGY

There are many more growth myths that you will run across. See how many you can identify. Here are a few more to consider:

- Developers just want to operate in a "free market."
  Reality check: Growth is heavily subsidized.

- Building more (and bigger) roads will solve the problem of traffic congestion.
  Reality check: Build it and they will come.

- Bigger (or more) is better.
  Reality check: Small is beautiful and enough is enough.

- Faster (or quicker) is better.
  Reality check: How much faster do you want to go?

- Change is good!
  Reality check: Change is inevitable, but not necessarily good.

THE TRUTH ABOUT JOBS, HOUSING, AND GROWTH

*What is the use of a house
if you haven't got a tolerable planet to put it on?*

— Henry David Thoreau[1]

Jobs, housing, and growth are integrally connected in many ways. New jobs attract new residents and create a demand for more housing. The salaries paid by those new jobs determine the kind of housing that is needed. Two of the most powerful growth myths are that we must keep growing in order to provide good jobs and that we must also grow to provide affordable housing. Although these myths are introduced in Chapter 3, there is much more to say about these two complex and important issues that are so strongly entwined with urban growth.

The desire by the public to provide jobs and housing has led to the use of subsidies in the form of economic development programs and publicly subsidized housing programs. When local governments spend money on these programs, they often end up inducing growth. This happens when people from outside the area are attracted by the prospects of good employment and low-cost housing. This is the simple reason why local job and housing programs often end up being growth subsidies that do not resolve local problems. The challenge addressed in this chapter is how to achieve community goals in both of these areas without subsidizing unwanted growth.

We start off by examining the jobs issue in more detail to expose some inherent flaws in traditional economic development programs.

Fortunately, there are alternative public investments that can foster economic prosperity while providing a broad range of benefits to the entire community. When new growth controls have been successfully implemented in your community, housing affordability may become the next big issue. It's a good idea to address housing up front during growth discussions and propose proactive solutions. Poorly designed public housing programs can end up costing taxpayers a bundle and encouraging growth by subsidizing home construction. The second part of this chapter presents some of the proven solutions to meeting the affordable housing needs of your community without big subsidies.

THE CATCH 22 OF GROWTH

A fundamental growth paradox applies to good jobs, affordable housing, and all other community amenities. It can be stated as follows:

The Catch 22 of Growth

The better you make your community,

the more people will want to live there,

until it is no better than any other community.

This Catch 22 is based on historical patterns:

- People will tend to re-locate to improve their situation.
  (This sort of migration of people in search of opportunity and improved conditions has been going on since history began.)

- People will continue moving to our town as long as conditions are perceived to be better here.

- People will stop coming only when overall conditions are no better in our town than they are elsewhere in the country.

People tend to move to wherever economic opportunities (job prospects) are best, but other factors can also play big roles — housing prices, quality of schools, safety, sense of community, recreational opportunities, other amenities, or an overall high quality of life that the community is perceived to offer.

What does this mean for dedicated civic volunteers, public officials, and urban planners? Will our efforts to make our community a better place to live only result in attracting more people? Will these people continue to come until their cumulative impact has eliminated any advantage our town may have had? Yes. In fact, this scenario has repeated itself countless times. We say these communities are "victims of their own success." The "success" may be good jobs in Silicone Valley (San Jose, California); a beautiful greenbelt in Boulder, Colorado; affordable housing in Las Vegas, Nevada; or the formerly clean, dry air in Phoenix, Arizona.

The main message of the Catch 22 of Growth is to emphasize the importance of controlling growth locally. Local efforts to provide jobs, make housing affordable, or improve the quality of life in a community are likely to have short-lived success unless they are also accompanied by growth controls.

Because the demand for good jobs and affordable housing is nationwide, the most effective solutions to meeting job and housing needs will be implemented at the national level. Thus, the federal government is the best agent for such programs. The federal role has been widely recognized for a long time and federal job-training and housing programs are the result. However, this has not prevented local governments from trying to seek their own solutions.

JOBS AND GROWTH

What's the Problem with Traditional Economic Development?

The Job Creation Paradox described in Chapter 3 — that creating jobs increases the number of people out of work — is essentially the same dilemma as the Catch 22 of Growth. It explains why it is so hard to solve local unemployment problems locally. The more jobs we create in our community, the more people will move here to snap them up. Job creation fuels growth and ultimately leads to a larger population of unemployed people.

There are few who would argue against the benefits of having decent jobs for those who need and want them. Jobs are essential in our society. Without them we are unable to gain access to essential goods and services and cannot participate in the benefits of our vast economy.

Jobs are so important that perhaps there should be a basic right to work. Yet we are still led to believe we must sacrifice our environmental quality, our natural resources, our public treasury and even our health for these jobs. Corporations tell us we must be willing to live with their pollution if they are to create the new jobs everyone wants. And we must give them cheap resources, hefty tax breaks, and free infrastructure or they threaten to locate elsewhere. However, while corporations might seek these benefits, they aren't necessarily the best ways to provide jobs.

We have become all too familiar with the exploits of some major corporations as they bid one locality against another to see which will offer the greatest subsidy package. Many economic development expenditures are little more than public "gifts" to the private sector. All too often, major corporations absorb huge tax subsidies while producing few tangible or quantifiable public benefits. A review of the literature on tax incentives for economic development conducted for the Oregon Department of Economic Development found "little evidence that they are effective in promoting economic development."[2] The report states:

> Economic development is often identified as the creation of jobs. If this is the goal, then it is seldom accomplished by the use of tax incentives. Further, to the extent that it is accomplished, it appears to generate a net fiscal drain when viewed from the state as a whole. Increasing development that leads to increasing population creates a demand for public services and infrastructure that is likely to offset any tax revenue gains.

The core purpose of economic development is typically to help create jobs for those people in the community who need them most — primarily the unemployed or underemployed. In many cases, economic development efforts are broadened to include improving salaries for the area's lower-income workers. However, economic development can stray far from its core mission when it is painted as broadly as improving economic conditions or diversifying and strengthening the local economy. Public resources may end up in dubious investments and speculative projects. Some economic development expenditures may be so poorly made that the community would be better off hauling the money to the local landfill.

Creating jobs sounds like a noble purpose that must certainly be worthy of our local tax dollars. But how noble is it when economic development programs fail to improve local employment conditions, end up subsidizing big businesses, and fueling unwanted growth? One problem is the "business first" philosophy of many economic development practitioners. They start by assuming that businesses create all jobs. Therefore, subsidizing business growth will lead to job creation. They conclude that more and bigger businesses will undoubtedly hire more people. This is also referred to as the "what's good for business, is good for people" philosophy. This approach ignores the fact that most companies are in business to make money not employ people. Their goal is to maximize revenue, while minimizing expenses. And employees are one of the expenses to be minimized.

A better approach is the "people first" philosophy. We start by assuming it is people who create and run all businesses. If we can accept the idea that businesses exist to serve the needs of people, then the question becomes "How can we get business to better serve the needs of all people?" The alternative philosophy that "what is good for people, is good for business" leads to some new strategies for economic development. But first, a few more points about traditional economic development.

It is likely to be unconstitutional for local governments to restrict the new jobs created by economic development to people living within their boundaries. They must accept applicants from anywhere in the country and they must hire the most qualified people that apply, not the most needy. In small communities, this means that many of the best new jobs will go to people from out of the area or out of state. Studies show that in the short term, 30-50 percent of new jobs go to in-migrants rather than the original residents.[3] In the long term, 60-90 percent of the jobs end up going to newcomers.

Economic development incentives from local governments frequently result in business subsidies that equate to a public cost of $15,000 to $50,000 or more per job created. While these per-job costs may sound expensive, they are higher still when calculated in terms of the number of jobs actually going to local workers. Take the case of the Hyundai semiconductor factory that was lured to Eugene, Oregon in 1995 by economic development officials who offered $40 million in tax credits and other subsidies. The factory will ultimately employ 800 people. This amounts to a subsidy cost of $50,000 per new job. But, according to the company's own information, only half of those hired were from Oregon. Even fewer were from Eugene, where the city's $40 million subsidy will be made up by its taxpayers. This means that subsidies are well in excess of $100,000 per original Eugene resident hired at the plant.

Paved with Good Intentions: Economic Development in Fort Collins, Colorado

In 1986, the City of Fort Collins, Colorado sought to create more jobs by attracting the Anheuser-Busch Brewery with a subsidy package valued at more than $50 million. Additional state and county subsidies were also offered in the successful bid.

In order to direct more of the new brewery jobs to local residents, potential applicants were required to pick up the necessary application forms in person. At least 56,000 people did so! (The total population of Fort Collins at the time was only 82,000.) Ultimately, 20,000 people submitted applications during the 18-month hiring period. Public agencies helped to screen the job applicants. About 15,000 were selected for "aptitude testing." By 1988, the brewery had 500 employees.

In a rare occurrence, the county kept records of where each new employee lived at the time they were hired. Only 133 employees (27 percent) out of 500 hired were residents of Fort Collins. Another 54 employees (11 percent of the total) were from outside the city but within the county. If the public subsidy offered by the city ($50 million) is divided by the number of jobs that went to city residents (133), the cost to local taxpayers was $376,000 per resident employed!

The Anheuser-Busch Brewery case illustrates two fundamental problems with traditional economic development subsidies:

- First, the jobs go to the most qualified applicants and the eligible pool includes everyone living in the U.S. Local residents often comprise a minority of the total hired.

- Second, the subsidies fuel growth by creating expectations for employment (i.e., 20,000 applicants for 500 jobs), attracting more people to the area than there are jobs to be filled.

Fort Collins learned a valuable lesson from their experience. The city now has a policy that economic development incentives aren't given unless a development can demonstrate through analysis that its benefits to the community are greater than the cost of any public subsidies. To aid in this analysis the city recently developed what may be the first computer model to evaluate local economic, fiscal, and environmental impacts of economic development investments.

The city's policy of weighing costs and benefits prevented Fort Collins from offering big subsidies to attract the Hyundai semiconductor factory that ultimately ended up in Eugene, Oregon. The Hyundai factory has been the source of large-scale citizen opposition in Eugene since the secret recruiting deal was announced in early 1995.

Should our local governments be in the business of buying local jobs? If so, how much is a local job worth? Certainly it would depend on the salary and stability of the job as well as whether or not a local person will fill it. But the idea of putting a price on a job is fraught with problems. We can assume that a good job has some value to the person it employs. If we assume further that a job may also have some value to the community, then wouldn't both new *and* old jobs have value? It would not make sense for a local government to spend money luring a new business to town while allowing another established business to move away or close down for lack of assistance. An existing job retained in the community would be just as beneficial as a new job created. In fact, a retained job might be more valuable than a new job because that company has already been integrated into the community and its economy. If this is the case, then all existing jobs are as valuable as new jobs. But local taxpayers can't afford to subsidize all local jobs. Under our economic system, jobs simply have to justify themselves.

Economic development programs often discriminate against local businesses in favor of luring new businesses. By providing tax credits and other subsidies to certain businesses and not others, such programs create an uneven playing field that acts to the disadvantage of the unsubsidized local businesses that must compete with a subsidized business for customers, employees, and office space.

Economic development dollars often go to companies paying barely more than minimum wage. The city council might consider low-wage jobs to be important entry-level employment, but consider the following: In the U.S., a household of three earning less than $17,850 ($8.58 per hour or 167 percent of minimum wage) qualifies for food stamps, public housing, and energy assistance. Even with an income of $28,600 ($13.75 per hour or 269 percent of minimum wage) this same household will qualify for subsidized housing and school lunch programs. While some communities consider any new job to be a good job, the fact is, recruiting low-wage jobs to a community can actually create a shortage of low-income housing and an increased demand for public assistance.

Multiplier effects are commonly used to justify economic development expenditures. The theory of the multiplier effect is that a new wage earner will spend his or her wages in the community. This increased spending is thought to create additional economic benefits in the community. Thus, according to the multiplier effect theory, a new dollar brought into the community in the form of a new payroll may actually have an equivalent benefit of two or three dollars.

If this were true, then a small town that grew into a big city would have reaped the benefit of so many multiplier effects that everyone would be awash in money. But this doesn't happen, so what's wrong

ASK QUESTIONS ABOUT ECONOMIC DEVELOPMENT

Here are some basic questions that should be part of any discussion of the issue, but seldom are:

- Who will get the jobs? (How many out-of-work locals will be hired?)
- What kind of jobs are they?
- What salaries will be paid?
- Will this business be stable and make a long-term contribution to the community?
- What will the full cost be to the community? (Include subsidies, infrastructure, services, environmental, and social costs.)
- Are the benefits to the community clearly greater than costs?
- What are the risks if the business should go bankrupt, move away, or simply not perform to expectations?
- What alternatives are there that might achieve similar benefits with fewer costs?

with this theory? The most likely reason we don't see such a fabulous accumulation of wealth over time is that communities are *open systems*. Goods and services come and go as the community is constantly trading with the rest of world. The more money the community has, the more money is spent on goods and services from outside. While some new businesses bring money into the community, others take it out. National chain stores, in particular, tend to sell goods produced outside the area and take profits back to the corporate headquarters. As a counterbalance to the multiplier effect, perhaps we should all become more familiar with this "divider effect."

Another issue with multiplier effects is which *effect* is being multiplied. While local spending might increase, does this mean the general welfare of the community improves? Have the average income levels been increased? Or have we merely increased the size of the local economy, attracted more people and generated more competition? The effect that is most certainly multiplied is growth. What remains uncertain is to what extent the general public benefits.

Rather than merely touting the benefits of economic development, wise local officials will consider the costs as well. If a thorough cost-benefit analysis accompanied all major public investment decisions, we could easily weigh the benefits of economic development subsidies against the direct costs and fiscal impacts of the resulting additional growth. Economic development expenditures should also face budget prioritization. How will this use of public funds stand up against the needs of schools, libraries, and public safety programs?

Investing in Real Economic Health

There must be a better way! We can start by rephrasing the question we are trying to answer: How do we foster a healthy local economy and help provide decent jobs to the people in our community who are out of work — and do it in the most cost-effective manner?

Recognizing that your community cannot be an island of prosperity and full employment, investments must be directed in ways that will help accomplish the above goal while primarily serving as broadly beneficial investments for the existing residents. Below are some alternative public investments that will promote the economic and social welfare of the community without unduly fueling unwanted growth:

- *Invest directly in local people.* Job training, job placement programs, good public schools, and adequately funded higher education benefit local residents directly.

- *Invest in the community.* A strong, livable, safe community with good neighborhood organizations and adequate parkland, recreational opportunities, community centers, and other public amenities will foster local business growth and generate a host of economic benefits.

- *Protect the quality of the local environment.* Clean air and water can be significant economic assets that benefit everyone.

- *Fill local governments jobs with local applicants.* Avoid actively recruiting new employees from all over the country, as many governments do. (The same applies to the hiring of local consultants and contractors.)

An important step in fostering real economic well-being is to recognize that all human wealth is ultimately derived from our natural environment. While this might seem obvious to many, it is still possible to get a Ph.D. in economics without ever using the word *environment*. Protecting the local environment is critical to the long-term economic welfare of a community. Here are some of the local investments that foster economic health through environmental quality:

- preserved farmland and forests for their economic and other benefits.

- undeveloped open space for aesthetics, passive recreation, and other values;

- wetlands and watersheds for flood control, water quality, and other values;

- scenic areas and attractive natural features that cannot be replaced;

- wildlife habitat and ecological diversity and quality maintained by a system of protected natural areas and wildlife corridors.

Instead of just more jobs, what we really want are good jobs without a host of negative impacts. The first step is to define the kinds of businesses you want in terms of the impacts you don't want. Again, take the example of the Hyundai semiconductor factory that was attracted to Eugene with tax credits, free infrastructure, and promises of cheap land, labor, water, and electricity. The factory uses ten times as much water and electricity per new job as the average employer in Eugene. The factory releases hundreds of tons of toxic chemicals into the air and water and has increased regional sewage effluent levels by ten percent. It consumed more than $1.3 million in capital equipment for each new job created and required one acre of land for every five jobs created. And, it pays less than the existing median salary for similar manufacturing jobs in the area.

We can stop using public resources to attract wasteful, polluting, low-paying, resource-intensive industries. The kind of business expansion most people want is clean and resource-efficient. It offers good salaries and uses a minimum amount of land, capital, and public resources for each new job created. These values can be reflected in objective standards or indicators that gauge the performance of an individual business or industry. The simplest benchmarks to use for these standards are the existing averages for local or regional businesses. We only want to attract or expand businesses that will raise the existing standards. Assuming that job creation is our goal, then appropriate standards would be based on minimizing negative impacts per job as shown in Figure 4-1 for environmental standards.

Louisiana State University Professor Paul Templet developed an environmental standard that was used briefly in that state as a criteria for economic development.[4] He found that an objective standard

Figure 4-1
Environmental Indicators for Economic Development

Category	Indicator
Resource Use	
• Water	gallons/day/job
• Land	acres/job
• Energy	kilowatt-hrs/job
Pollution Emissions	
• Hazardous/ toxic waste generation	pounds/year/job
• Solid wastes	tons/year/job
• Sewage effluent	gallons/day/job
• Air emissions	pounds/year/job

based on a chemical emissions-to-jobs ratio could be used effectively to qualify facilities for tax exemptions in Louisiana. The standard, based on annual pounds of chemical emissions per job, focuses attention on two of the state's goals: lower emissions and more jobs. (Chapter 6 has more on setting standards for growth.)

Some people express concern that keeping a polluting industry out of their town just forces some other town to deal with it. While this may be true, standards have to start somewhere. The more towns that restrict pollution emissions, the more likely state and federal governments will be to adopt tougher standards and the more incentive these industries will have to use more-efficient manufacturing techniques and to maximize recycling and waste reduction.

If local government officials insist on extending economic development subsidies to businesses, the subsidies should be generating clearly defined public benefits. An example of such a subsidy would be a tax credit that rewarded any business (not just certain big businesses) that created a permanent new job and hired a local, unemployed individual to fill it. If subsidies are targeted to any particular class of businesses it should be locally owned, small businesses, that actually create more than 90 percent of the new jobs in our economy.[5] Why not suggest some guidelines and minimum standards for business subsidies? Think in terms of the kinds of businesses you want in your community. The environmental indicators in Figure 4-1 can be combined with social and economic criteria to define the kinds of businesses that will contribute to the community. For example, any business seeking tax subsidies, special favors, or some other form of public assistance could be required to meet at least the following minimum standards:

- Offer median salaries that are higher than the existing median for local workers in the same industry. Too many economic development funds are used to lure companies that actually "lower the bar" for local salaries. (*Median* means half are above and half are below. This is a better measure than *average* salaries because average salaries can be inflated by a few highly paid executives.)

- Produce less pollution per worker than the average of existing businesses.

- Use less of the area's natural resources per worker than the average of existing business. This means less land is consumed for each job created and fewer gallons of water and fewer kilowatt-hours of electricity are required per worker.

- Use fewer hazardous and toxic chemicals than existing business.

- Minimize waste products through recycling, reuse, and most-efficient production practices.

- Have minimal negative impacts on the community in terms of traffic, noise, parking, aesthetics, and general livability.

- Agree to return any public subsidies if the business moves out of town or closes within the first five years of beginning operation.

The most desirable businesses would also be worker friendly. They would provide good benefits, training or educational opportunities, involve employees in company policy and decision-making, have employee profit sharing, agree to limit the proportion of temporary workers hired, not be anti-union, and maintain a good worker safety record. (Note that the above criteria would not necessarily apply to businesses choosing to locate in your community without public subsidies.)

HOUSING AND GROWTH

The issue of affordable housing often becomes the "Achilles heel" for growth management. The argument put forth by the real estate development industry is that growth controls will restrict housing supply and push prices up. As explained in Chapter 3, the issue is really much more complex. Growth pressures will tend to force up housing prices whether or not any growth controls are in place. Nevertheless, this argument has been used like a wedge to break apart local land use plans and growth management policies.

While the availability of affordable housing is always a legitimate concern, it must be kept in perspective. Home ownership in the U.S. was at an all-time high at the end of 1997, with two out of three households owning the homes they live in. As described in Chapter 1, society continues to expand its definition of housing needs as new homes become bigger and the number of occupants in them shrinks. The legitimate realm of local government is to help ensure that everyone's most basic needs are met — not that rich and poor alike can enjoy cheap, publicly subsidized housing. Also, it is important to recognize that new housing is not the only source of affordable homes. Only 15 percent of all homes for sale nationally are new. The remaining 85 percent are the resale of existing homes.

According to the Catch 22 of Growth, a desirable town facing growth pressures cannot remain an island of affordable housing in a sea of demand. So what can communities actually do to ensure an adequate supply of low- and moderate-income housing? Affordable housing is such a vague term that it could mean almost anything. Start by defining what aspects of housing and housing affordability are of public concern and setting priorities. Initial priorities might be to provide:

- adequate temporary shelter space for homeless individuals and families in our community;

- publicly subsidized housing for those living at or near the poverty level; and

- a reasonable supply of low- to moderate-income housing.

Even when we limit ourselves to the most basic housing programs, we still have to answer the question of how much is enough? When will we have provided enough shelter space and low-income housing? While there is no set method for determining the proper mix of housing, a community's housing objectives should not be open-ended. The availability of shelters and low-cost housing can actually attract people from outside the community. One town cannot expect to solve the housing problems for the entire region. However, it is possible to estimate what a responsible, reasonable, or fair share of low-income housing might be. The answer could be based on local demographics for household incomes in the area. This information would help determine what percentage of the housing inventory would need to be affordable to lower-income households. In cases where local demographics are atypical (very wealthy or very poor), it may make more sense to base a "fair share" of low-income housing on state or national household income distributions. Alternatively, housing needs could be based on salaries paid by local businesses.

County wide or state wide housing programs tend to be much more equitable than city-based programs because they address a larger region and distribute the burden of funding such programs more fairly. A common problem with market-driven housing construction is that builders tend to build for the top end of the market because there is more profit in high-end homes than in economy homes. This can leave a community with an inadequate supply of moderately price homes. A good affordable-housing program will include incentives or requirements to ensure that new construction generates a desirable mix of housing.

There are some good methods for providing adequate low- and moderate-income housing without resorting to the kind of subsidies that cause more growth. They include inclusionary zoning, linkages, community land trusts, flexible residential zoning, and others.

Inclusionary Zoning

Inclusionary zoning is a requirement that new residential development include a certain percentage of low- and moderate-income housing. This helps ensure that a desirable mix of affordable housing is created as the community grows. Inclusionary zoning is widely used, achieves the intended results and, in most cases, doesn't require direct public subsidies. A 1995 survey of inclusionary housing programs showed that they are found all across the U. S. but are most popular in California, where they are used in 45 cities and have produced 20,000 housing units.[6]

A typical inclusionary housing program applies to residential development projects of at least five to ten housing units. Smaller projects may be required to pay into a city housing fund instead. A minimum amount of the new housing (usually ten to 25 percent) must be available for designated categories of low-income housing (very low-, low- and moderate-income housing). Inclusionary requirements apply to both rental and for-sale housing.

Some programs only require that the affordability be maintained for ten or 15 years. After that time the housing reverts to market conditions and the affordability is usually lost. This forces the community to constantly replenish its supply of affordable housing. It can also create a situation where the property owner receives a hefty, unearned profit as the house reverts to market value. The best programs create a perpetual supply of low-income housing. The affordability criteria are maintained in perpetuity through deed restrictions, legally binding agreements, and resale restrictions. Burlington, Vermont and Davis, California are two cities with good inclusionary programs that have created a permanent inventory of affordable housing.

Mandatory inclusionary requirements are often combined with incentives to keep the cost of building below-market-rate housing from being overly burdensome to developers. Density bonuses, for example, are an incentive that allows a developer to build ten to 20 percent more housing on a given area of land than existing zoning would otherwise permit.

Figure 4-2
Example of Inclusionary Housing Program Requirements

Category of Affordability	Household Income as a Percent of Median Household Income	Required Housing Units in Category
Very Low Income	Less than 50 %	5%
Low Income	50 - 80 %	10%
Moderate Income	80 - 120 %	10%

Jobs-Housing Balance (Linkages)

Commercial development that creates new jobs also creates a need to house the employees. A hotel, for example, will create many low-wage service jobs. The hotel workers may be forced to seek low-cost housing in distant suburbs or outlying communities. Jobs-housing *linkages* can be used to help ensure that workers have nearby housing they can afford. Linkages require that the commercial developer either contribute to an affordable housing fund or build suitable nearby housing commensurate with the income levels of the jobs created. The linkages help create a balance (or "link") between residential and commercial land uses and reduce automobile travel. Linkages are widely used in California and the Northeastern United States. In Aspen, Colorado linkages enable service industry workers to live in the extremely expensive community that depends on their labor.

Community Land Trusts

Community Land Trusts (CLTs) are increasingly being used to provide affordable housing. They are also widely used to preserve farmland and open space (see Chapter 6). The CLT is typically a nonprofit, charitable organization that acquires land and uses it to create permanently affordable housing. By taking the land out of the speculative market, the trust insulates the property from future price escalation. The CLT controls the type of housing that is built on the land and may lease the land at very low rates to developers who are willing to build housing that meets criteria established by the trust. As a tax exempt organization, the trust can receive charitable donations and convey tax benefits to the donors.

Flexible Residential Zoning

Many residential zoning and building codes are unnecessarily rigid. They allow only single-family homes with one kitchen and with minimum building setbacks from lot lines. This approach has some virtues such as creating a simple and consistent system for avoiding conflicts with neighbors. However, it may prevent the expansion of a house or the use of accessory dwelling units that are contained within the structure of the house. Accessory units and apartments within larger houses can provide economical housing without the impact of building a new home or apartment building. Mixed-use zones allow for residential development to be combined with commercial development in convenient and economical ways. There is the potential for flexible zoning to create conflicts with adjoining neighbors. If such conflicts are anticipated, they can be addressed through a design review process that involves neighbors and seeks their approval.

Development Impact Fee Credits and Other Incentives

More and more communities are using *development impact fees* to pay for some or all of the cost of providing the many public facilities required to serve new development — roads, parks, schools, libraries, sewage treatment, and so forth. (Development impact fees are discussed in more detail in Chapters 5 and 6.) These fees can be implemented in a flexible manner that lets the community create incentives for the kinds of development that meet important public goals, such as providing affordable housing. Other affordable housing incentives include financing assistance, increased density levels, reduced standards, density transfers, and streamlined approval processes.

The employment and housing solutions presented in this chapter are intended to show that a community's future need not be hitched to unfettered growth. In fact, the lack of growth controls contributes to these problems and ensures that they will be perpetuated. The more growth, the more jobs and housing the community must provide. The more jobs and housing the community provides, the more growth occurs. By adopting growth controls, it is possible to meet these important public needs more effectively, while at the same time protecting and improving the qualities you value in your community.

DISCOVERING THE REAL COST OF GROWTH IN YOUR COMMUNITY

*Once, citizens automatically accepted the idea that growth —
in numbers of people, in jobs, in industries — would ease the
public burden by increasing the tax rolls and spreading per
capita costs. Now they have doubts. They seem to be expressing
the belief that larger size reflects not only lesser quality but
also higher costs. Pressed by inflation, they listen carefully to
arguments about the hidden costs of growth.*

*The new mood reflects a burgeoning sophistication on the
part of citizens about the overall, long-term economic impact
of development. Immediate economic gains from job creation,
land purchases, and the construction of new facilities are
being set against the public costs of schools, roads, water treatment plants, sewers, and the services new residents require."*

— William K. Reilly, *The Use of Land,* 1973

Most of us who have been exposed to rapid urban growth can
testify to its negative impacts on our lives and our surround-
ings — lost open space and environmental quality, overcrowded schools, traffic congestion, noise, rising crime rates, higher
cost of living, and so on. Few of these costs have ever been quantified
in a useful way. Even the straightforward economic costs associated
with growth, such as providing new or expanded public facilities, are
relatively unknown. While the benefits of growth are widely proclaimed,

information about growth-related costs is surprisingly scarce. This lack of knowledge is of particular concern given the magnitude of public investments necessary to accommodate growth.

This chapter is not intended to provide a balanced discussion of the possible costs and benefits of growth to the public, but merely to improve the understanding of the cost side of the equation. However, one unequivocal benefit of urban growth is the increased diversity that tends to exist in a bigger community. Larger communities have a greater selection of theaters, stores, and restaurants. They likely have a wider range of cultural opportunities. A larger community will tend to have a greater variety of jobs due to its more diversified economy. However, the variety of jobs does not mean that employment is any easier to obtain. It means that if your professional skills are highly specialized, your chances of finding compatible employment may be better in a big community than a small one.

While not everybody values diversity, many value it highly. Some of the best cities to live in are those that have achieved a fairly high level of diversity while remaining small. These cities often have educational or cultural centers that foster diversity. A community can also encourage diversity, without growing, by actively supporting small businesses, entrepreneurship, cultural activities, fairs, festivals, musical events, and so forth.

It may be helpful to start off this chapter with a conceptual framework for evaluating growth costs. The realm of growth impacts can be broken into three main areas: economic, environmental, and social. Growth has real and significant costs in all three of these areas. Economic costs are the main focus of this chapter because they are easily documented and quantified with readily available information. Also, economics is often the primary basis for making decisions in both the private and public sectors. Economic costs tend to carry more "weight" than environmental or social costs in today's decision-making processes — even though the actual value of these other costs might be higher. To further focus the discussion of costs, the economic costs can be divided into public sector and private sector costs. Public sector costs are those paid by taxpayers to fund the services of government, while private sector costs are paid by buyers and sellers in the marketplace.

The first part of this chapter reviews some of the best available literature on the cost of growth. The second part of the chapter looks at how much growth is likely to be costing your community. Examples of how to do your own growth cost estimates are provided. The chapter concludes by addressing the question of equity or "who should pay for growth?"

What's Been Said About the Cost of Growth?

Most of the professional literature on the cost of growth has dealt with the issue of sprawling development patterns. The most comprehensive analysis of growth costs is the famous *Cost of Sprawl* study conducted in 1974 by the Real Estate Research Corporation.[1] This study used a range of typical "prototype" development scenarios as the basis for estimating costs. It evaluated a full range of costs, including direct capital costs, operation and maintenance costs, environmental impacts, and livability/quality-of-life impacts. The study found that it costs substantially more to serve sprawling residential development than it does to serve compact development closer to a city center. Sprawling development was found to use more energy, generate more air pollution, have greater environmental impacts, and require more capital costs for roads and utilities.

Another important cost-of-growth study is the 1986 *Density-Related Public Costs* by the American Farmland Trust (AFT).[2] The AFT

Source: Roger Lewis, courtesy MSM Regional Council, used with permission.

examined public costs and revenues associated with a range of residential development densities in Loudoun County, Virginia. They found that the annual cost of providing public services was 43 percent higher for sprawling development (one unit per five acres) compared with compact development (one unit per quarter acre). When the total tax revenues from residential development were compared with the public costs of serving it, there was a net shortfall in each case. According to the report, "The results of this analysis show that over a wide range of densities the ongoing public costs of new residential development will exceed the revenues from such development." Figure 5-1 shows that the annual net revenue shortfall per new house was found to be three times greater for sprawling development ($2,232) than for compact development ($705).

The AFT has repeated this type of cost of community services in 11 other locations around the country and consistently finds that residential development creates a net fiscal burden on the community.[3]

But aren't there some cases where growth does generate a fiscal sur-

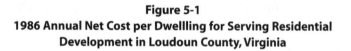

Figure 5-1
1986 Annual Net Cost per Dwellling for Serving Residential Development in Loudoun County, Virginia

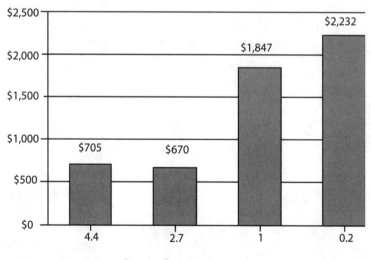

Density (houses per acres)

Source: American Farmland Trust, 1986.

Figure 5-2
Fiscal Impact By Land Use in Redmond, Washington, 1997

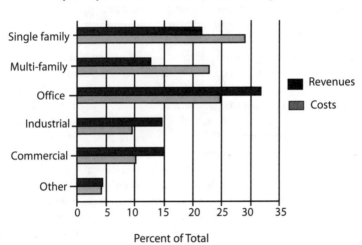

Percent of Total

Source: City of Redmond Phase Two Report.

plus for the region? Yes. In some instances, certain kinds of commercial development will result in a net revenue gain to the community. Figure 5-2 shows the results of a detailed analysis of costs and revenues for major land uses in Redmond, Washington.[4] While residential uses cost more to serve than they generate in revenues, commercial uses generate a net surplus for the city. These results are entirely dependent on the existing tax and fee structure that generates the revenues in the first place. They may also depend on how we define the "region."

The standard explanation for the fiscal advantage of some commercial development is that it is typically taxed at a similar property tax rate as other types of development (based on a percent of assessed value) but requires less public infrastructure (capital facilities) and services. While in some cases commercial development may have a positive revenue impact on the growing urban center where it occurs, it can also have very negative fiscal impacts on surrounding "bedroom" communities. These communities often house the workers for the commercial centers. The surrounding local governments are burdened with providing a full range of residential infrastructure and services, but they receive none of the tax revenues from the commercial center. Some metropolitan areas have used regional revenue sharing to resolve these inequities.

Returning to the cost-of-sprawl question, an AFT study of California's Central Valley (1995) showed that, compared to a sprawling development pattern, more compact, efficient development would save 500,000 acres of farmland from development and save local cities $1.2 billion by the year 2040.[5] Another major study conducted in New Jersey in 1992 by Robert Burchell and his colleagues at Rutgers University evaluated the costs and benefits of alternative growth scenarios.[6] The researchers found that well-planned growth would save the state $1.3 billion in infrastructure costs over 20 years compared with the current development pattern. While the New Jersey study evaluated physical infrastructure requirements and cost-of-growth data, the purpose was to compare alternative development patterns and not to compile a complete set of growth-related costs. A similar cost-of-sprawl study by Burchell performed in Michigan in 1997 found that, "Compact growth saves 3.5 percent in annual local public sector services costs."[7] On the whole, studies on the cost of sprawl tend to show that compact, well-planned growth consumes about 45 percent less land and costs 25 percent less for roads, 20 percent less for utilities, and 5 percent less for schools.[8]

Most of these studies focus on demonstrating the relatively higher costs of lower-density, less-planned development. Cost-of-growth data itself is a secondary finding of these studies. However, each new development creates public costs for infrastructure *regardless of its density and design.* True, some developments cost considerably less than others, due to good planning, good site design, good building design, higher density and proximity to utilities, public services, and transportation corridors. Still, the public costs of growth remain high and some major costs, such as those for school facilities, are largely independent of density. Thus, while sprawling development remains a major concern, growth itself has a high public cost that needs to be addressed independent of *how* we grow.

The net cost of growth is evident in two significant studies that examined the relationship between growth and increasing taxes. A study by the DuPage County, Illinois, Planning Department in 1991 found that new development causes property taxes to go up.[9] Areas in the county with faster growth had higher tax increases. This implies growth has a net public cost that tends to manifest itself in tax increases. A similar, but broader, 1995 study by the Metropolitan Planning Council representing the greater Chicago area looked at the fiscal impacts of growth in the six-county region surrounding Chicago.[10] This study found that population growth tends to increase the residential tax burden. Fast-growing areas that did not raise taxes tended to see a reduction in public services. This last conclusion alludes to the fact that there are other ways the public sector pays for growth in addition to raising taxes.

The costs of growth to local government can manifest themselves in five ways: increased taxes; increased debt (usually as municipal bonds); infrastructure deficit; facility maintenance deficit; and a reduction in public services. The first two expenses, increased taxes and debt, are costs most people are familiar with and are the traditional means of funding public facilities and services. The third cost, infrastructure deficit, results when a community falls behind on providing the new and expanded facilities needed to accommodate growth. This cost takes the form of overcrowded schools, congested roads, and overflowing sewage plants. Facility maintenance deficit results when the funds needed to maintain public facilities are diverted to meet the immediate needs of new development. This shows up as an inability to pay for the basic maintenance of local public buildings, roads, parks, and recreation facilities. The final growth cost area shows up as a reduction in the quality or extent of public services. As with maintenance deficit, the needs of new development can divert public funds away from providing basic services. Library hours may be cut back, community centers closed, and school programs eliminated.

An earlier study conducted by the Santa Fe, New Mexico, Planning Department in 1973, reinforces the conclusion that growth costs the public more than the revenue it generates.[11] The report states:

The primary conclusion of this study is that new subdivisions do not pay their own way as far as the public economy is concerned. Higher density development is less burdensome per unit than is lower density development, since a subdivision which encompasses a smaller area is less expensive to provide with services.

The deficit incurred by residential units is not unique to Santa Fe. There are few communities where residential developments actually cover all the costs for services provided them ...

Residential and supporting commercial development, wherever it occurs in and around the city of Santa Fe, incurs a deficit in the public economy and consequently creates a financial burden that is eventually borne by the taxpaying public.

Case Study: The Cost of Growth in Springfield, Oregon

The town of Springfield grew rapidly during the 1970s. The 1970 population of 27,000 increased 55 percent to 42,000 by 1980, amounting to an average annual growth rate of 4.5 percent. A study done by Springfield's Planning Department, called *The Cost of Growth: 1971-1981*, found that ten years of rapid growth had left city finances decimated.[12] Total municipal spending quadrupled (in constant dollars) over this period. Total indebtedness also quadrupled to pay for new bond issues. Thus, while the city population grew 55 percent, its expenses and debt had both grown 300 percent. On a per capita basis, city spending had tripled. Such increased expenses and debt are typical of communities facing rapid growth and struggling to provide costly new facilities and services.

So far, all of these studies demonstrate that growth can create net public costs, but they don't tell us precisely how these costs originate. A number of studies from around the country show that the cost of providing public infrastructure — water, sewerage, drainage, police, fire, library, school, park, recreation, and other community facilities — adds up to anywhere from $20,000 to more than $30,000 for an average new single-family house.[13] This cost increases substantially for sprawling, low density development. It is important to note that these figures are for off-site costs and *do not* include the local streets and utility connections that are part of a subdivision's development costs.

New developments of all kinds — residential, commercial, and industrial — create demands for costly new infrastructure. A new school might cost $10 million; a new fire station, $7 million; a road upgrade, $15 million; a sewage plant expansion, $100 million. These expenses can place a continual burden on existing residents who end up paying for them in their tax bills.

To fully understand how much growth costs, it is helpful to know a little more about how growth-related costs are paid. As shown in Figure 5-3, revenues for local governments include property taxes, other taxes, and other revenue sources such as fees and permits. As growth occurs, these revenues tend to increase with the size of the community. There are three basic cost areas for local government shown in Figure 5-3. The first two, operation and maintenance, can be grouped together as "O&M" and represent the general ongoing costs of providing government services. (Maintenance includes all repairs to existing facilities, including repaving streets, mowing parks, and fixing roofs.) The third cost area is capital construction and represents the cost of building

Figure 5-3
Fiscal Impact Analysis
Comparison of Development Revenues and Costs

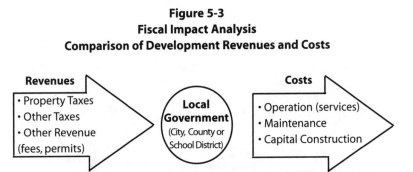

new or expanded public facilities. These facilities, also called public *infrastructure*, include new roads, new school buildings, police stations, community centers, land acquisition for parks and open space, new sewage treatment plants or any other public facilities. Capital construction or infrastructure costs include both new facilities and the expansion of existing facilities to increase capacity. Growth will tend to increase O&M costs and capital construction costs for local government. However, since studies show that growth tends to create a net fiscal burden, the increase in overall costs must be higher than the increase in revenues.

It can be difficult to distinguish growth-related costs from other public costs. For example, when a new park is built, how much of the cost of the park should be attributed to growth and how much should be attributed to the needs of the existing community? Developers often say that since everyone can use the park, everyone should pay for it. To understand how these costs can be reasonably allocated, start by examining the differences in public expenditures between two hypothetical scenarios: a non-growing or stable, community; and a growing community. These two scenarios are illustrated in Figure 5-4.

In the first scenario, the *stable city* has had a fairly constant population for some time. All the necessary public facilities — roads, schools, fire stations, parks, and government facilities — have already been built and paid for. These facilities are adequate to meet the needs of the community. Taxes are still being collected in the stable city, and public revenues are paying for the ongoing O&M expense of government. However, there is no need to expand or build additional facilities as long as existing facilities are properly maintained. Some facilities will wear out and need to be replaced. These facility replacements (such as a new heating system for a school) are part of the O&M budget.

Figure 5-4
Two Scenarios for Evaluating Growth-Related Costs

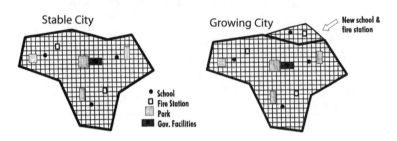

However, if the stable city becomes a *growing city*, there will be additional costs to build new or expanded facilities to supply the increased demand resulting from new growth. These capital construction costs are clearly growth-related costs because they did not exist in the stable city scenario. Each increment of growth creates an incremental increase in demand for physical infrastructure.

When the costs for new facilities are paid through property taxes (as with a general obligation bond issue), they are spread across the entire community. If the area of new growth in the growing city of Figure 5-4 represents about ten percent of the total population, then these new residents will pay only ten percent of the cost of the new facilities required to serve them. The other 90 percent will be paid by the existing residents. In this manner, existing residents continue to pay a greater share of new infrastructure costs required to serve new development. The more the city grows, the greater the burden on existing residents.

Note that the new school and fire station shown in Figure 5-4 may be shared by the entire community. Nonetheless, the need for these facilities did not exist in the stable city scenario because the existing facilities were already adequate. This illustrates why most, or all, of the costs of these new facilities are correctly attributed to growth. Also note that both stable and growing scenarios have O&M costs that vary in rough proportion to the size of the population. Property tax revenues will increase, to some extent, to match the increasing O&M costs of a larger community.

Figure 5-5 shows the major categories of growth-related costs. The first column lists the basic public infrastructure costs that have been the focus of this chapter. Each of these infrastructure categories

Figure 5-5
Growth-Related Costs

**Capital Costs for
Public Facilities/Infrastructure**

- School Facilities (K-12)
- Sanitary Sewer System
- Storm Drainage System
- Transportation System
- Water Service Facilities
- Fire Protection Facilities
- Parkland & Recreation Facilities
- Police Facilities
- Open Space
- Library Facilities
- General Government Facilities
- Electric Power Generation and Distribution
- Natural Gas Distribution System
- Solid Waste Disposal Facilities

**Environmental Costs
and Other Impacts**

- Decreased Air Quality
- Decreased Water Quality
- Increased Rates of Resource Consumption (water, energy, etc.)
- Increased Noise
- Lost Open Space and Resource Lands (farms and forests)
- Lost Visual and Other Natural Amenity Values
- Lost Wildlife Habitat
- Increased Regulation (loss of freedom)
- Lost Mobility Due to Traffic Congestion (delays and increased commute time)
- Higher Cost of Housing
- Higher Cost of Living
- Increased Crime
- Lost Sense of Community
- Costs to Future Generations

requires an incremental increase in capacity to serve each new development. There are straightforward procedures for calculating how much capacity each new development requires and how much it will cost to provide that additional increment. Even though these costs can be calculated fairly easily, no local government has yet done a complete job of it. Some of the most complete studies, described later in the chapter, address only those categories of infrastructure funded by the city itself (rather than by a school district or utility district).

The second column in Figure 5-5 lists environmental costs and other impacts. While these costs can be substantial, they can also be difficult to quantify in terms of dollars. However, economists are developing methods for valuing environmental and social costs. When more thorough cost accounting has been done, we may find that the environmental and social costs of growth are even greater than the economic ones.

In 1995 I was asked to give a presentation on the cost of growth to a land use conference in Oregon. Because I could find so little information available on this topic in Oregon, or anywhere else in the U.S., I decided to compile data myself using standard methods of fiscal impact analysis. The cost figures were updated and published in a 1996 report called "The Real Cost of Growth in Oregon."[14] A summary of these costs in Figure 5-6 shows that the price of infrastructure for only seven of the above categories totaled $24,500 for a typical new single-family house. Note that schools were by far the most expensive facility required by new development and accounted for 48 percent of the total. Transportation facilities and sewage systems were the next most expensive.

Several recent municipal studies have also evaluated growth-related costs for various categories of public facilities. The City of Boulder, Colorado has a policy of requiring development to pay for growth-related impacts on public facilities. In order to help implement this policy, the city conducted a comprehensive evaluation of seven categories of development impacts: library, municipal facilities, fire, police, parks and recreation, transportation, open space, and affordable housing.[15] This is one of the few studies to examine the cost of providing library, fire, and police services. The study did not, however, include school facilities or utilities such as water, sewerage, storm drainage, and energy. The costs were carefully allocated between residential and non-residential (commercial and industrial) development impacts, as

Figure 5-6
Cost of Public Infrastructure
New Single-Family House, Oregon, 1996

Cost Item	Amount
School Facilities	$11,377
Sanitary Sewerage	$5,089
Transportation Facilities	$4,193
Water System Facilities	$2,066
Parks and Recreation Facilities	$797
Stormwater Drainage	$510
Fire Protection/EMS Facilities	$470
Total	**$24,502**

Figure 5-7
Fire Service Calls By Land Use in Boulder, Colorado

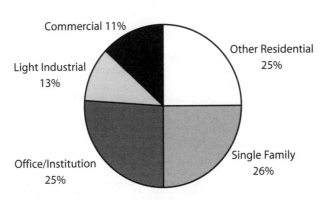

Source: Boulder Fire Department.

shown in the example for fire service in Figure 5-7. In this case, single-family and other residential land uses accounted for about half of all fire service calls. Thus, half of the cost of a new or expanded facility would be allocated to residences. Careful allocation of costs ensures that any fees that may be charged to new development are equitable.

Figure 5-8 summarizes the impacts for the seven categories of public infrastructure evaluated. The number of occupants in a house will influence the demand for public facilities like roads, parks, and libraries. New single-family houses in Boulder were assumed to have an average of 2.7 occupants per household. Other types of housing, such as townhouses or apartments, were assumed to have 1.9 occupants per household. The total cost of providing public facilities for a new single family house in Boulder is $16,323. Non-residential costs were allocated on a per-square-foot basis and are not directly comparable to the residential costs.

The total public facility costs would have been considerably higher had the analysis included Boulder's schools and utilities such as sewers, water, and stormwater drainage. These costs were not included in the study because they are handled with separate fee systems. (Schools have their own excise tax on new development and utilities are funded through hookup fees charged by the city.) The high cost of parks and open space reflects the city's commitment to parkland and outdoor

Figure 5-8
Cost of Development Impacts on Public Facilities in Boulder,
Colorado, 1996

Public Facility Category	Residential (cost per dwelling)		Non-Residential (cost per 1000 sq. ft. of floor area)		
	Single Family Detached	All Other Housing	Light Industrial	Commercial /Shopping Center	Office / Institutional
Library	$427	$301	$160	$160	$190
Municipal	$446	$313	$90	$90	$110
Fire	$107	$87	$80	$100	$220
Police	$132	$92	$10	$70	$20
Parks & Rec	$4,306	$3,030	$1,090	$1,100	$1,320
Transportation	$7,378	$5,091	$5,080	$25,450	$8,640
Open Space	$3,527	$2,482	$870	$880	$1,060
Totals	**$16,323**	**$11,396**	**$7,380**	**$27,850**	**$11,560**

recreation and its extensive greenbelt system of open space.

This analysis guided Boulder officials in developing a proposal to increase development charges in the form of a development excise tax. However, even though the proposed schedule of charges was reduced substantially from the full costs identified in the analysis, Boulder's voters rejected the proposal at the polls in November 1997. One possible reason is that the proposal fell under Colorado's constitutional requirements that all new tax measures be clearly labeled as a tax increase. Voters may have viewed the ballot measure as a tax increase rather than a shift of funding intended to achieve greater equity. In addition, the measure lacked organized public support to balance opposition from several business groups.

How Much is Growth Costing Your Community?

Each community has different standards for public facilities and different costs for land, construction materials, and labor. Each will have its own system of taxes and fees to pay for new facilities. For these reasons, local cost and revenue data should be used whenever possible. However, when such data is not available, the next best source may be regional, state, or even national data. Construction costs for most cities in the U.S. are within 20 percent of the national average. Only the bigger cities like Los Angeles and a few other places such as Alaska have costs outside this range. Cost figures for other locations or other years can be adjusted, when necessary, using engineering cost indexes such as *Means Construction Cost Data* or *National Construction Cost Estimator* to give reasonable, current estimates for costs in your community.

Due to the complexity of public finance, it is always desirable to have the local government provide accurate and complete information on the costs and revenues associated with growth in your community. When this is not possible, citizens may want to make their own estimates. This section explains the principles and methods for assessing growth costs. Examples are provided to help you calculate four different categories of infrastructure: schools, transportation systems, sewers, and water supply. Other types of infrastructure can be calculated in a similar manner. Even if you don't plan to make these calculations, reading through examples will give you a better idea of how growth costs can be objectively determined.

The following examples calculate the full public-sector cost for providing service capacity to a typical new single-family house. The costs here are not necessarily net costs. In other words, they do not reflect credit for any payments, such as *impact fees*, that may be made by developers towards these costs. Any such payments should be deducted from the costs calculated here, to arrive at a net cost. The single-family house is a common unit of urban growth, however similar calculations can be made for office buildings, quick-marts, grocery stores, and every other type of development. School facility costs are typically allocated entirely to residential development, since that is what creates the demand for school capacity. Commercial development, especially retail, is likely to create a high demand for transportation facilities due to the volume of automobile trips it generates.

We can use a "proportionate share" costing method to determine the public infrastructure costs associated with the construction of a typical single-family house. The approach is simply to apportion a reasonable share of costs across the user base. Each increment of growth is then charged only for the increment of system capacity required to serve it.

The starting point is to clearly define the unit of growth for which we wish to calculate the costs. This example uses a representative three-bedroom, single-family house on a modest 6,000 square foot lot (see Figure 5-9). It is assumed that the house is part of a larger development or subdivision that is located in an urban area on previously undeveloped land with nearby utilities. This hypothetical house is representative of the compact urban development that has a minimum

Figure 5-9
Profile of Hypothetical New House

Characteristic	
House Size	3 Bedrooms
Lot Size	6,000 sq. ft.
Land for Streets (21% of lot)	1,260 sq. ft.
Development Density	6 units/acre
Occupancy:	
Total Persons	3.1
School-age Persons	0.67

Source: Occupancy and public school-age children per house is the national average based on the American Housing Survey for a three-bedroom house from Burchell, 1994.[16]

cost for urban services. The house is assumed to have 3.1 occupants – the national average for a new three bedroom house. Use local demographic data for new housing when it is available.

To simplify accounting, we assume all infrastructure requirements are met with new facilities. However, most communities have at least some excess capacity in their public infrastructure. If we meet the needs of new development with existing excess capacity, we can estimate the value of the existing infrastructure and assign it to the development in the same manner as new infrastructure. Frequently, existing excess capacity is valued at *replacement value,* which is essentially the same as new facility costs.

In most cases, growth-related costs are independent of the actual residents of the house. Owners and occupants of a particular residence may come and go, but on the average, we must assume that each new house comes with a statistically representative set of occupants. Therefore, it is the construction of the house itself that creates the additional capacity requirements for public facilities and other impacts on the community. There are some special situations such as retirement housing that do not generate demand for new schools.

Finally, note that while these examples calculate the public cost associated with growth, not all of these costs will be paid by *local* taxpayers. Some public works projects receive federal and state contributions. Thus, the full public cost may differ from the local community's cost. It should be easy to determine how much of the cost is paid with local funds. There are also instances in which developers provide public amenities or other contributions that mitigate the net cost of their development to the community.

School System Costs

Schools are the single most expensive cost item associated with new development, yet the growth-related cost of schools is rarely calculated by the school districts that must provide the facilities. Rapidly growing communities usually find that a shortage of school capacity is the first big problem they face. Voters may be willing to occasionally approve $10 to $20 million in bonds for new school construction, but fast-growing communities need new schools every year and the taxpayers may decide they have paid for enough schools. School districts can easily calculate the cost of providing school facilities to serve new development. The national average for a three bedroom house is 0.67 public school-age children. Thus, there will be an average of two school-age children for every three houses (3 x .67 = 2). A new 750-unit subdivision will require the equivalent of one new school for the 500 students that can be expected to move in (750 x .67 = 500).

School construction costs should include all expenses required to produce a completed school, including planning, designing, engineering, and building, as well as the cost of equipment and land. If the total cost for a school with a capacity of 600 students is $13.5 million, then the cost of capacity per student is $22,500 ($13,500,000/600). If there are 0.67 school age children per house, then the cost per house is $15,075. Note that this is not a cost per child! It is the cost to create the permanent school capacity required to serve the permanent demand created by new houses and the people who will inevitably live in them.

An example of a more sophisticated analysis of school costs can be performed using the extensive data provided in the New Jersey study mentioned earlier.[17] As shown in the last column of Figure 5-10, the 1992 capital costs for New Jersey schools range from $13,860 per elementary school student to $25,740 for a high school student. The per-student costs can be linked to a new home by determining the number of school-age children likely to be living in the home at each grade level (see Figure 5-11). The resulting average cost of providing new school facilities for each new home is $11,377.

Transportation

A common method for determining the cost of transportation systems (streets, roads, bike paths, and transit) related to new growth is based

Figure 5-10
School System Capital Cost Example per Pupil

School Levels (Grades)	Elementary (K-6)	Middle (7-9)	High (10-12)
School Building Area (square footage/pupil)	120 sq.ft.	150 sq. ft.	180 sq. ft.
Construction Costs ($/square foot)	$105	$115	$130
Construction Costs ($/pupil)	$12,600	$17,250	$23,400
Land Cost per Pupil (at 10% of construction cost)	$1,260	$1,725	$2,340
Total Cost Per Pupil	$13,860	$18,975	$25,740

Source: *Impact Assessment of the New Jersey Intirim State Development and Redevelopment Plan.*

Figure 5-11
School System Capital Cost Example per New Three-Bedroom

School Levels (Grades)	Elementary (K-6)	Middle (7-9)	High School (10-12)	Total K-12
Total Cost Per Pupil	$13,860	$18,975	$25,740	
Number of School-Age Children per New House	0.42	0.13	0.12	0.67
Weighted Cost $/house	$5,821	$2,467	$3,089	$11,377

Source: *Development Impact Assessment Handboook.*[16] Public school-age children per house is the national average based on the *American Housing Survey* for a three-bedroom house. Note that from two to 15 percent of school-age children may attend private schools, reducing public costs accordingly.

on level of service (LOS). The first step is to establish a standard LOS for the city or county. The most reasonable basis for this standard is the current level of service. The LOS may be measured in terms of total vehicles per day or a standard level of acceptable congestion during a peak hour. In this manner, each additional travel demand requires additional infrastructure in order to maintain the existing level of service. For example, the city of Woodburn, Oregon uses its average traffic count on two-lane arterial and collector roads — 6,000 vehicles per day — as its LOS standard for calculating traffic impact fees.

Each new development generates a certain number of new trips. The Institute of Transportation Engineers publishes *Trip Generation*, a manual that lists typical trip generation rates for various land uses. An average single-family home generates 9.55 trips each weekday. Half of these trips are allocated to the residence and half to the destination (office building, store, etc.). The residence, therefore, is credited with 4.78 trips. The U.S. Department of Transportation has conducted trip length surveys showing that the average length of a trip from a residence is 2.25 miles.

Multiplying the number of new trips generated by the average trip length gives the total additional miles traveled, or 10.75 miles. The cost of building a mile of two-lane arterial or collector road in Woodburn is $2,340,000 (in 1993 dollars). This cost includes land for the right-of-way, two travel lanes, on-road bike lanes, sidewalks, curbs, storm drains, street lighting, and all design and engineering costs. The cost attributable to a new house is equal to the cost of 10.75 miles of new road, divided by the 6,000 total vehicles sharing it. This works out to $4,193 per new house. Because some of the roads in the city are funded by the state, 72 percent of this cost, or $3,020, is the city's cost for providing transportation infrastructure. Woodburn's current traffic impact fee collects only 29 percent of the total cost, or $876 per new singl-family house.

Another method of calculating transportation system costs is to base them on long-range transportation plans. For example, Washington County, Oregon (next to Portland) calculated the cost of the new roads that will be needed to serve projected growth over a 15-year period. The county also calculated the amount of residential, commercial and industrial development that was expected to take place over this time. The cost of these transportation system improvements were allocated to the projected new development based on the number of vehicle trips each kind of development would generate. The cost per new residence was determined to be more than $6,000. The county's current $1,790 traffic impact fee covers only part of that cost.

Sewage System Costs

The City of McMinnville, Oregon completed a new sewage plant in 1996 intended to serve the city's projected total population of 37,000 in the year 2015. The cost for the entire project, including system expansion

Figure 5-12
Cost Allocation For Sanitary Sewer Infrastructure
in McMinnville, Oregon, 1995

Cost Item	Cost ($millions)	Percent Allocation to Growth*	Cost to Growth ($millions)
Plant construction cost	$29	43%	$12.5
Planning, design & construction management	$8	43%	$3.4
Repair, upgrade, infiltration (not capital improvements)	$22	0%	$0.0
Collection system expansion	$17	100%	$17.0
Debt service (present value)	$24	43%	$10.3
Total cost	**$100**		**$43.2**

* The 43 percent figure is the ratio of new residents (16,000) to total projected residents (37,000).

and repairs, was $100 million.

McMinnville's population was 21,000 at the time the project was started in 1995. It is projected to grow by 16,000 new residents over the next 20 years. The first step is to allocate costs between current and future residents. As shown in Figure 5-12, $43.2 million of the total can be attributed to new growth.

According to McMinnville's City Engineer, 61 percent of the sewage plant capacity can be assigned to residential usage (with 34 percent to commercial and five percent to industrial usage). The total cost to the 16,000 future residents is $26.4 million (0.61 x $43.2 million). This works out to a cost of $1,647 per person. Based on an average of 3.1 occupants in the household, the cost of new sanitary sewer facilities per house is $5,100.

The cost of providing sewer service can increase by $5,000 to $10,000 per new house for low-density sprawling development that requires longer runs for sewer mains.

Water System Facilities

The capital costs associated with providing potable water include water supply costs (water rights, wells, and other acquisition costs), filtration plants, storage reservoir capacity, and the distribution system.

The Eugene Water and Electric Board (EWEB) in Oregon performed a study in 1996 to evaluate the capital costs for adding new customers to the water system.[18] This study determined the incremental capital costs associated with adding a new residential water meter to the system.

The calculation performed by EWEB considers the value of both the remaining excess capacity and new (or planned) capacity. In 1996, the excess capacity of the existing system was 6.3 million gallons per day (mgpd) and was valued at $10,991,000. The utility's capital improvement program estimates a need for 6.2 mgpd additional capacity by the year 2010. Expansions and capital improvements associated with this additional capacity were estimated to be $18,571,000. These two costs were then combined to give the total capital cost required to serve new customers from 1996 through 2010.

Available peak capacity (excess plus new) is then distributed across the maximum number of residential water meters that can be served under peak demands. The equivalent of 14,000 new residential meters can be served with approximately $29 million in capital facilities, resulting in a cost of $2,066 per new house.

ENVIRONMENTAL AND OTHER COSTS

The environmental and social impacts of growth tend to be more visible than the economic impacts and also tend to generate the most opposition. Traffic congestion, pollution, lost open space, increased crime rates, lost sense of community, and reduced quality of life and livability top the list of problems caused by growth. Economists refer to these types of costs as "external costs," or "externalities," because they are external to the market pricing system. While externalities do have very real costs, they do not appear on any economic balance sheet or in any supply-and-demand pricing relationship.

If the environmental and social externalities of growth could be put in monetary terms, they might very well exceed the fiscal impacts. Methods for monetizing environmental and other external costs are becoming increasingly used and accepted. Research in this area represents a challenging opportunity for ambitious economists. Unfortunately, while this research appears to be a worthwhile endeavor, the truth is that even the readily assessable economic costs of growth are poorly understood and greatly in need of further study.

The one cost of urban growth we may not be able to put a price on is the impact on future generations. The losses of open space, farmland, scenic vistas and natural settings are permanent and all future generations will be deprived of their benefits.

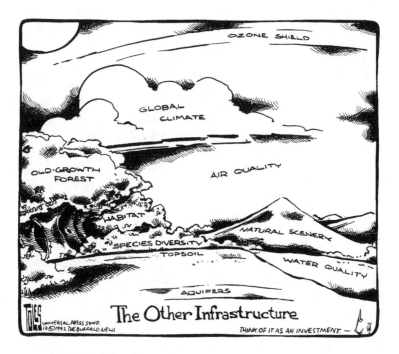

TRACKING DOWN THE COST OF GROWTH IN YOUR COMMUNITY

You can often identify some of the growth costs in your community
using available public information. Start by identifying all the possible
sources of local growth-related cost information. You may be in great
shape if your city, county, regional council of governments, or school
district has recently analyzed future infrastructure costs. If not, most
local governments generate a "capital improvement plan" or "capital
facilities plan" that lists the anticipated expenditures for new and
expanded public facilities for the next five to ten years. These plans are
based on growth forecasts and are updated on a regular basis to help
the local government project and budget costly capital projects. They
typically cover all the infrastructure categories for which that government or district is responsible: schools, roads, sanitary sewers, storm
drainage, parks and recreation, water service, municipal facilities, open
space, and so forth.

Thurston County, Washington, where the city of Olympia is located, is projected to grow from its 1997 population of 197,000 to nearly 360,000 by 2020 — an 85 percent increase. A group of citizens in the Olympia area were concerned about the cost of this growth and how taxpayers would pay for it. Calling themselves the Carnegie Group, they made use of a 1997 regional infrastructure financing report issued by the local regional planning council and did their own cost-of-growth analysis.[20]

There is increasing appreciation among the urban Americans of the fact that, however warranted it might be on some grounds, continuous metropolitan growth carries with it certain obvious cost to the quality of life.[19]

— Santa Barbara Planning Task Force, 1974

The report they used compiled data for the first time from numerous local communities on the regional infrastructure funding needs and revenue sources. The report covered a six-year period from 1997 to 2002 and included all major categories of public infrastructure (general government, parks, schools, sewers, solid waste, stormwater, transportation, water, and special purpose districts for fire and flood control). It broke all costs for each type of infrastructure into three main areas (see Figure 5-14):

- catch-up costs: expenditures needed to bring facilities up to existing standards;

- keep-up costs: expenditures to maintain, repair and replace existing facilities; and

- new capacity costs: expenditures to accommodate growth and new demand.

In order to estimate the actual cost of growth to taxpayers, the Carnegie Group assigned all new capacity costs to growth. Keep-up costs were not included in their analysis, since these costs are really ongoing O&M costs for existing facilities. The proper allocation of catch-up costs was more complicated. These expenditures primarily make up for past growth where the region fell behind in providing adequate facilities (infrastructure deficit). Also, the state's 1990 Growth Management Act initiated new requirements for communities to set standards for public facilities. Some of the catch-up expenses were needed to bring service levels up to the new standards. Such costs are not growth-related expenses. The Carnegie Group recognized that catch-up costs were a gray area, but they lacked the data necessary to accurately allocate them. They decided to allocate these costs to

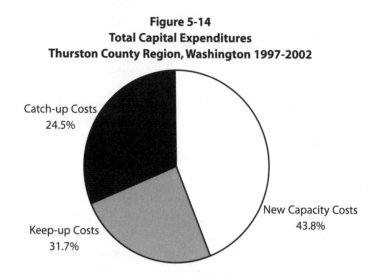

Figure 5-14
Total Capital Expenditures
Thurston County Region, Washington 1997-2002

Catch-up Costs
24.5%

New Capacity Costs
43.8%

Keep-up Costs
31.7%

growth for several reasons. First, they believed that the non-growth component of catch-up was very small. Second, they compensated by overestimating the contribution new development makes to offset these costs by subtracting all road fund revenues from the cost total. These assumptions were made necessary by a lack of sufficient data. This happens quite often in the complex field of fiscal impact analysis. Rather than let this prevent them from educating the public about growth costs, the group chose to clearly explain their calculations and assumptions in their literature.

To arrive at a net cost to taxpayers, the Carnegie Group subtracted all revenues generated by growth from the total cost associated with growth (new capacity and catch-up costs). For informational purposes, this net cost was put on an annual basis and divided by the number of taxpayers in the county to arrive at an average annual cost per taxpayer of $600. The message was clear in their illustration (see Figure 5-15): taxpayers are subsidizing growth. This was the first time residents of Thurston County had a reasonable estimate of how much growth was costing them.

At least partly as a result of this work by the Carnegie Group, the City of Olympia is proposing to raise development impact fees. The group has also presented the city with a draft ordinance that would require a fiscal impact analysis of city council decisions.

In another example of growth-cost accounting, Steve Pomerance, a former Boulder, Colorado, city councilor and former board member of the Denver Regional Council of Governments (DRCOG), analyzed the regional transportation costs for the Denver area. He used the DRCOG's *2020 Regional Transportation Plan* (1997 draft) as a source for growth projections and associated transportation system costs.

Pomerance focused his analysis on the regional system costs and ignored local transportation costs. In this manner, he could be certain all costs were incurred by the public sector (taxpayers), rather than by developers or homeowners paying for local subdivision roads. The regional costs included major streets and roads (arterials), highways, and transit. The total cost for regional improvements needed between 1995 and 2020 to maintain existing level of service is $11.4 billion. According to the DRCOG, this estimate includes only roads and transit facilities that are likely to be built, and therefore is not inflated by costly "wish list" projects. The expenditures are needed to prevent "vehicle hours of delay" from increasing significantly and will not improve existing congestion levels.

System expansion costs were allocated between existing residents and new residents. System expansion costs resulting from existing residents come from a projected 12 percent increase in the amount of vehicle travel per capita (measured as vehicle miles traveled per person or VMT/person). This increase in driving by existing residents accounts for roughly 25 percent of the total VMT increase by 2020, with the remaining 75 percent resulting from forecasted population growth.

The increased travel of existing residents was subtracted from the total projected increase in travel by the year 2020. This leaves the total

Figure 5-15
The Cost of Growth In Thurston County, Washington

FIRST BANK OF ENDLESS GROWTH
Thurston County Branch   *January 1, Every Year*

Pay to the Order of *Thurston County Treasurer*

Five hundred and ninety-six dollars and 50/100   **$596.50**

           annual taxpayer contribution for
For *infrastructure to accommodate growth*

Your Signature Here!

Source: The Carnegie Group. Reprinted with permission.

cost required to meet the travel needs of new residents at $8.29 billion. By dividing the total cost by the 682,000 new residents anticipated, Pomerance determined that the regional transportation-system cost per new person is $12,151. (It was not possible to assign these costs to particular types of development because DRCOG did not allocate trip generation by these categories.)

Clearly the costs associated with providing transportation facilities for new growth in the Denver area is very high. The next question, though, is to what extent the new growth pays this cost and to what extent it is subsidized by existing residents. Using current sources of revenues, system costs would be paid almost entirely by general taxes and user fees (impact fees and developer exactions make a very small contribution to costs at the regional level). Both general taxes and user fees can result in subsidies by existing residents paying for infrastructure needed to serve growth. Available information was not adequate to calculate the subsidy precisely, but Pomerance estimates that new development will pay less than 20 percent of the transportation system costs it creates. Therefore, the per capita growth subsidy is more than 80 percent of the $12,151 cost, or about $10,000 for each new resident.

WHO SHOULD PAY FOR GROWTH?

Awareness about the high costs of growth often leads to a great deal of confusion about who should pay these costs, and how. *Development impact fees* are an increasingly popular method of paying for the infrastructure required by growth. This "pay as you grow" approach requires that development pay the estimated cost of the infrastructure it will require in order to obtain building permits.

Development impact fees (discussed in more detail in Chapter 6) tend to create a more equitable distribution of growth-related costs. Without such fees, existing residents of the community are constantly subsidizing people who move into the community later. Nonetheless, recovering the full cost of development remains controversial. The issues and questions are fairly predictable.

Developers and pro-growth advocates often argue that growth infrastructure subsidies should be continued since existing residents were also subsidized at some point. This is undoubtedly true, however inequitable subsidies in the past do not justify continued inequitable subsidies. Your community can get off the subsidy treadmill while maintaining fair treatment and allocation of all public infrastructure costs.

Developers may then argue that some of the new homes are purchased by people who have lived in the community for a long time and have already paid for their share of infrastructure. While this might sound reasonable, it is actually irrelevant to the cost accounting for growth. The costs we have described in this chapter are a result of the new home (or new office building) being built. The public facilities must be in place to serve the new development *regardless of who owns or leases it*. Assume, for example, that a family who has lived in the community all their lives buys a new home. According to the developers' viewpoint, this family has already made its contribution and should not pay again. But what if the family decides the house was not suitable and moves again in two years? This time someone from out of state buys the house. Should this new homeowner now pay the fees that were waived for the local family?

Finally, it is argued that growth benefits the community and therefore deserves to be subsidized. The benefits are said to include increased revenues from property taxes, sales taxes, income taxes, and increased business revenues. As we have seen, increased tax revenues are often not sufficient to offset the increased costs of serving new growth. While certain private businesses and individuals in the community may benefit from growth, the real question is whether the community as a whole benefits. The best way to resolve questions about the costs and benefits of growth is through better information and analysis. If growth really does produce broader benefits, it should be possible to document them in an objective analysis performed by the local government.

Private sector benefits from growth could be documented with a *cost-benefit analysis* that considers both sides of the equation in terms of the economic impacts on local residents. In addition to using an economic cost-benefit analysis, the local government can perform a *community impact analysis* that provides broader and more complete information on a given development proposal (see Chapter 6 for more on this). By doing a community impact analysis, the community can make much more informed decisions about major new developments.

So far, even cities that know how much growth is costing have found it politically impractical to charge new development the full cost of all categories of infrastructure. Instead, they charge a fraction of the full cost, or charge full cost for only a few types of infrastructure. This may change with greater awareness and understanding of growth costs.

Putting the Brakes on Growth — What Works?

True growth is the ability of a society to transfer increasing amounts of energy and attention from the material side of life to the nonmaterial side and thereby to advance its culture, capacity for compassion, sense of community, and strength of democracy.

— Arnold Toynbee

U rban growth occurs incrementally, one office building or sub-division at a time. As a result, it is often difficult for people to recognize the adverse impacts growth may be causing in their community. It can be even harder to respond to this incremental growth with the kind of major policy initiatives that may be necessary to protect the community from these impacts.

A one percent annual growth rate is often considered to be quite modest for urban areas. After all, this has been the average population growth rate for the U.S. in recent times. One percent growth might be a reasonable rate for a short period of time, but consider what this would mean over the long term:

Question: If we were to go back to the year 10,000 BC, not long before the earliest agriculture, and start with just two people, what would the population of the Earth look like today if the population increased at one percent per year?

Answer: The Earth would be a solid ball of human flesh with a diameter greater than the size of our solar system and a radius expanding outward faster than the speed of light![1]

Amazing as it may sound, this example is mathematically correct. It's clear that modern growth rates are vastly greater than historic rates and are certainly not sustainable in any long-term sense.

One way to generate appreciation for the consequences of growth in your community is to anticipate change over a longer time frame. By projecting current trends into the future, it is easier to see the eventual results of current actions. Most cities plan for at least the next five years. Some plan for 20 years. There are even some good examples of 40- and 50-year city and regional planning efforts. But the average North American will be on this planet for slightly more than 75 years. Urban growth rates of two, three, or four percent per year may sound paltry now. But when considered over a human life span, they result in astonishing levels of growth many of us would not want to see.

Dr. Albert Bartlett, a physicist and expert on exponential population growth, frequently asks fellow residents this question about his home town of Boulder, Colorado: How big do we want Boulder to be in 70 years? At zero percent annual growth, of course, Boulder would remain the same size. But at historic growth rates, Boulder will become the size of our largest American cities (see Figure 6-1).[2] At a six percent per year growth rate, in 70 years Boulder would become as large as New York City was at the 1990 census. While this growth rate may sound extreme, Boulder actually grew at this average rate for two decades (1950-1970)! This puts rates of growth into some perspective. Since Boulder residents did not want their town to become the size of New York, they became proactive and developed some of the best growth controls of any U.S. city (see Boulder case study later in this chapter).

There are many effective solutions for managing and controlling growth. Selecting the right method(s) depends on the desired outcome and the level of public support that can be expected. This chapter begins by examining some of the many subsidies that tend to fuel growth — the growth "accelerator pedal." Reducing or eliminating these subsidies will relieve some of the growth pressure in your community and can result in a more equitable use of public resources. While this may be a logical place to start, there are many more policy options for citizens seeking to rein in unwanted growth. The second section on "applying the brake" presents some of the best techniques for controlling growth with fiscally and socially responsible policies. The

Figure 6-1
Boulder Tomorrow?
— Take Your Choice ...

By Professor Albert A. Bartlett
Steady Rate of Growth Required for Boulder to Become a Major U.S. City
in 70 Years

Comparable City Size	Population from 1990 Census	Boulder's Required Average Annual Growth Rate
Miami	358,548	2.08%
St. Louis	396,685	2.23%
Denver	467,610	2.46%
Boston	574,283	2.76%
Detroit	1,027,794	3.59%
Philadelphia	1,585,577	4.21%
Houston	1,630,533	4.25%
Chicago	2,783,726	5.01%
Los Angeles	3,485,398	5.33%
New York	7,322,564	6.39%

Reprinted with permission.

final section explores ways you can foster greater public awareness of growth impacts and develop support for successful new growth policies.

The term *growth management* is used broadly to refer to the various policies and regulations that can be used to guide growth and development. These range all the way from actively encouraging more growth to limiting or stopping growth. Most of the professional literature on growth management has focused on how to accommodate growth with fewer adverse impacts, sometimes referred to as "smart growth" or simply "planned growth." This literature on planned growth suggests policy approaches that are not intended to hinder growth, but rather to direct it in ways that minimize its negative impacts. These are clearly important policy options since, in the near term, most communities will continue to grow.

But many communities are ready to take the next step. They have already planned for, and accommodated, enough growth. They are now seeking ways to actively discourage it. This chapter will focus on those approaches to growth management that have the potential to moderate or restrain growth (slow it down) rather than accommodate it. These approaches are generally referred to as *growth controls*, rather than the broader term *growth management*.

TAKING THE FOOT OFF THE ACCELERATOR PEDAL

Before seeking to discourage growth in some manner, a community should do its best to not actively encourage it. Like driving a car, we should first take our foot off the accelerator pedal before we begin to apply the brake. Trying to restrain growth, while at the same time offering subsidies to new development, can send a very mixed signal to developers, the real estate industry, and the general public.

Growth incentives and subsidies are often buried in municipal budgets or are otherwise difficult to identify. Figure 6-2 summarizes some of the most likely places to look for the *public sector,* growth-inducing activities most communities engage in. These growth stimulating activities include economic subsidies, tax subsidies, below cost services, free infrastructure, relaxed regulations, and others. The second column of Figure 6-2 suggests growth-neutral policies to reduce or eliminate the growth incentives.

Surveys indicate that most people do not support growth subsidies that are ultimately borne by taxpayers. Adopting growth-neutral policies, as shown in Figure 6-2, is a way to get local government out of the business of stimulating growth. Greater public accountability and oversight of local development programs and budgets will also help reduce or eliminate these growth inducers. Some subsidies may perform useful public purposes. In such cases, the "burden of proof" should be on the subsidy to demonstrate a net public benefit.

There are also *private sector* growth inducements, among which *speculative development* is chief. A developer embarks on a project based on his or her speculation that there is a demand for a certain kind of development — an office building, industrial park, or residential subdivision. These developers gamble substantial investments, assuming they know the market and can predict the demand for their product one or two years in the future.

Speculative developments are often the last thing a community needs. All too often the result is a big new office building with no tenants or a subdivision without home buyers. However, by the time the project is completed, the developer and the banks that financed the project are heavily committed to its success. They will go to great lengths to market the project to potential tenants or buyers all over the country. These promotional campaigns are also taken up by the local

Figure 6-2
Ten Common Growth Subsidies and
Corresponding Growth-neutral Policies

Typical Growth Subsidies/Incentives	Growth-Neutral Policies
Infrastructure	
Free or subsidized public infrastructure to serve new development, such as new or expanded roads, sewer systems, water systems, schools, fire stations, libraries, etc.	Use development impact fees to recover the full costs for all types of public infrastructure required to serve new development.
Economic Development Programs	
Most traditional economic development programs are designed to promote growth. They include a wide variety of tax subsidies and grants to new and expanding businesses, free employee training, free city consulting services, and many more programs used to stimulate business growth	Terminate costly economic development programs that canno clearly demonstrate a net public benefit.
Developer Incentives	
Examples include selling city-owned land to developers below full market value and public-private development partnerships where the public ends up with the short end of the stick.	Require: • greater public accountability. • property value appraisals before sale. • competitive bids. • public cost-benefit analysis for joint partnerships.
Development Services	
Not charging the full cost of processing building permits, reviewing plans and performing inspections.	Charge full cost for all city development services.
Land Use Planning	
Much of local government staff work on urban land use and transportation planning are part of the process of planning for and accommodating growth.	Let new development pay for growth-related planning activities.

Figure 6-2 (continued)
Ten Common Growth Subsidies and
Corresponding Growth-neutral Policies

Typical Growth Subsidies/Incentives	Growth-Neutral Policies
Regulations	
Waiving environmental and land use regulations, or failing to enforce them, helps attract new industry at the public's expense.	Apply local regulations evenly.
Land Use Changes	
Rezoning land to allow developers to make more money off their projects ("windfall" profits)	Local governments can recapture developer windfalls created by the public sector through negotiated concessions.
Affordable Housing Programs	
Poorly designed affordable housing programs can end up being big public growth subsidies that are a boon for residential developers.	Avoid directly subsidizing home construction. Use regulatory approaches like inclusionary zoning and others described in Chapter 4. Try direct rent or mortgage payment assistance to low income families. Use existing housing stock rather than building new homes. Avoid programs where the city becomes a developer.
Federally-subsidized Road Building	
Many of the big road and bridge projects that encourage growth and sprawl are funded primarily by Federal taxpayers.	Learn to say "no" to Federal money.
Tax Increment Financing Districts	
TIF districts were created in the late 1960s and 1970s to channel local tax dollars to blighted downtowns. They exert a preemptive priority on the use of public funds for business and infrastructure expansion.	Phase out these districts. Stop making new TIF investments and pay off existing bonded debt.

GROWTH SIGNIFICA

• Number of U.S. communities that have successfully put an end to growth: none.

• Status of growth controls in the U.S.: Still in the experimental stages.

• Growth management "silver bullet:" Unknown.

economic development agency, the chamber of commerce, the local tourism department and sometimes even the city's planning and development department. The net effect of all this promotional hoopla is more growth, requiring more subsidies.

The following section on "Applying the Brake" provides more information on some of the growth-neutral strategies such as development impact fees, adequate public facilities requirements, and restrictions on speculative development.

APPLYING THE BRAKE

After we remove our foot from the accelerator pedal, what can we do to actually slow or stop growth? There are dozens of effective ways to manage and slow growth. Growth can be restrained temporarily or permanently, as long as there are valid public welfare concerns being addressed by the process.

In the U.S., the authority of local government to regulate growth comes from the Tenth Amendment to the U.S. Constitution that grants states the *police power* to regulate themselves. This same source of authority is used to enforce local zoning and building codes and environmental regulations. It is the right and obligation of the community to protect and promote the public health, safety, and general welfare of the public. The U.S. Supreme Court has consistently supported the right of communities to enact reasonable regulations for this purpose. The right to protect the health, safety, and welfare goes a long way and even includes matters of aesthetics. For example, regulations requiring compatible house paint colors in a neighborhood are likely to be upheld in court if they are carefully designed with the welfare of the general public in mind.

While there is a strong legal basis for growth controls, they are frequently challenged in court by development groups. If they are not properly designed, they will be thrown out (wasting lots of hard work!). To ensure that it survives legal challenges, an effective local growth ordinance must meet the following five criteria:

• comply with state and local law;

SURVEYS SHOW SUPPORT FOR GROWTH CONTROLS

A 1995 Colorado statewide survey shows the public wants development to pay its own way. [3] In response to the following questions, the public voted as follows:

Several ideas have been proposed to attempt to control growth. Would you support the following?

	YES	NO
Placing limits on the construction of new homes or businesses?	54.4%	45.6%
Imposing additional fees on developers to offset the public costs of growth?	69.0%	31.0%
Having state or regional agencies play a greater role in coordinating local growth plans?	59.3%	40.7%

- not violate the constitutional "right to travel";
- not be an actual "taking" of property;
- not be "exclusionary" (excluding any particular class of persons); and
- include findings to the effect that the proposed growth control is needed to protect and promote the health, safety, and welfare of the community.

The *right to travel* is an implied right based on the equal protection clause of the Fourteenth Amendment of the U.S. Constitution. This right assures freedom of movement about the country. According to one legal analysis, "Attempts to claim that growth-limiting land use ordinances violate the right to travel, beginning with the Petaluma case, have generally not been successful. The legal reasoning has been that if resettlement is indirectly made more difficult, but not prohibited, the fundamental right to travel has not been violated."[4]

It is best to start the local process of adopting growth controls by clearly stating the public goals (or benefits) that will be achieved by slowing growth. (Public goals are usually developed by the local leg-

PUBLIC SUPPORT FOR DEVELOPMENT IMPACT FEES

A 1996 Oregon survey of registered voters in five rapidly growing counties shows public support for development impact fees:[5]

If local public schools are at their capacity, should a city or community be allowed to charge builders and developers for the cost of building new schools?

Yes:	58%
No:	33%

When growth and development comes to a community or area, new infrastructure and services are needed, things like roads, sewers, water supplies, fire, police, libraries, and schools. In your opinion, who should pay for the cost of services created because of the new development — current residents of the area or developers and new home buyers?

Current residents should pay:	9%
Developers and new home buyers:	66%
Both should pay:	24%

Would you favor or oppose legislation in Oregon that would allow local governments to charge development fees to pay for more of the costs of services and infrastructure created by new development?

Favor measure:	75%
Oppose measure:	18%

islative body through a public involvement process or as part of a comprehensive plan.) These could include reducing the cost of growth to taxpayers, improving public health (clean air and water), lowering the cost of living, improving safety, increasing mobility, etc. List these goals and document them, if possible, as part of the local decision-making process. Based on a survey of all the cities and counties in California, preserving quality of life is the most commonly cited reason for enacting growth measures in that state (see Figure 6-3). However, this is a vague term, so you should identify the key elements that make up your community's quality of life.

Growth regulations frequently need to address conflicting public goals and balance different priorities. For example, the desire to prevent sprawl and preserve farmland or open space may affect housing affordability by limiting the supply of buildable land. Try to anticipate such conflicts and respond to them in advance. The solution in this example might be to propose a new funding source to help low-income residents with housing costs.

Occasionally there are statements that growth controls are elitist policies enacted by rich white communities. But the survey of growth measures in all of California's 443 cities and counties shows no racial or income class pattern in the enactment of the many growth controls in that state.[6] Communities with growth controls did tend to have better-educated residents, however. Another frequently voiced objection to growth controls is that they are intended to exclude lower income households. But the survey showed that the contrary is true. Cities that enacted growth controls also enacted more affordable housing incentives than cities without growth controls.

Strategies for Controlling Growth

There are dozens of growth controls that have been used successfully and there are undoubtedly many more waiting to be invented and tested. No single growth control technique is a panacea for all the problems growth pressures can bring. But the real question is not whether a growth policy is perfect. It's whether a proposed growth control is bet-

Figure 6-3
Reasons for Enacting Residential Growth Measures
Survey of Local Governments in California

Reason	Number of Times Reason Cited by Local Administrators
Quality of life preservation	98
Reduction in traffic congestion	93
Sewer capacity limitations	82
Water capacity limitations	63
Preservation of sensitive environmental areas	55
Open space/ridge line protection	51
Rapid population/housing growth	46
Limitation of urban sprawl	46
Agricultural land preservation	38
Air quality	38
Water quality	37
Quantity of high density housing developments	35
Quantity of low income housing developments	14
Other	58

Source: From a survey of 443 California jurisdictions with 907 growth-management measures, reported in *Regional Growth ... Local Reaction*.[7]

ter than the current policy (or another alternative). A good growth policy should result in broadly distributed, long-term benefits to the community.

Local growth controls can have spillover effects. When there is strong growth pressure, growth controls in one community may force growth into another nearby area where such controls don't exist. This is one of the strongest arguments for using a regional approach to growth management. Portland, Oregon's Metro is an example of an effective regional planning agency that coordinates growth among 24 different local governments in the Portland metropolitan area. Its success is attributed, in part, to the fact that it is the only regional government in the U.S. whose council officers are directly elected by the public. Other regional governments are run by appointed councilor who may be less accountable to the public they serve.

The growth controls summarized in Figure 6-4 and described in more detail below have been selected based on the following criteria:

- potential to moderate growth;

- potential to protect the community from various adverse consequences of growth;

- potential to improve quality of life and economic equity for existing residents; and

- likely to be both effective and practical in the current legal and political environment.

Development Impact Fees

Development impact fees are an increasingly popular means of funding the many types of public infrastructure required by growth. At least 18 states have now adopted *enabling legislation* that specifically authorizes local governments to collect these fees. With a system of impact fees, developers and new home buyers (or commercial building buyers) must pay more of the full cost of their impact on the community. Without impact fees, the existing residents of a community pay most of these costs through higher property taxes.

Properly designed impact fees charge new developments only for a *proportionate share* of capital costs. In this manner, each increment of new development pays only for the increment (or proportion) of new or additional capacity required to serve it. Unless limited by state law, local governments can charge impact fees for providing the following

Figure 6-4
Summary of Selected Growth-Management Techniques for Moderating Growth and Protecting Land

Slowing Growth	Preserving Undeveloped Land
• Development Impact Fees	• Public Land
• Setting Standards for Growth	Acquisition/Conservation
• Growth Rate Limits	Easements/Purchasing
• Capping Ultimate City Size	Development Rights
• Adequate Public Facility	• Transferrable Development
Requirements	Rights
• Urban Growth	• Community Land Trusts
Boundaries/Greenbelts	• Public Land Banking
• Annexation Restrictions	• Open Space Requirements
• Downzoning	• Conservation Tax Incentives
• Design Review/ Public Review	• Exclusive Agricultural Zoning
Process	
• Community Impact Statements	
• Environmental Impact Statements	
• Tax and Economic Incentives	
• Growth Moratoriums	
• Other Possible Growth Controls:	
1.Infrastructure Spending	
Restrictions	
2.Limiting Speculative	
Development	
3.Consumption Limits	
4.Carrying Capacity Limits	
5.Ecological Footprints	

new or expanded facilities: schools, roads, sewage treatment, stormwater systems, water supply, parks and open space, recreational facilities, police stations, fire stations, libraries, and other government facilities that must be expanded to serve new growth. These fees can be applied to all types of development (residential, commercial, and industrial). Courts have consistently upheld all reasonable and properly designed development impact fees.

Developers often argue that impact fees increase the cost of housing. This can be misleading since all the costs associated with housing remain exactly the same. The question is who pays them. Impact fees shift more of the cost burden from the general public (taxpayers) to the new home buyer who receives the benefits. Thus, impact fees are a matter of economic fairness or equity.

The potential benefits of impact fees include:

- **Lower taxes.** Impact fees reduce the burden on the general fund (tax base) and the need for more bonded debt by paying for growth-related infrastructure up front. This frees up public resources, which can be re-invested in the community or used to lower taxes.

- **Better market price signals.** The market economy operates more efficiently when pricing reflects the true costs of new development. Hidden public subsidies can send inaccurate price signals to the housing and development industry.

- **Incentives for good development.** In situations where low-income housing is needed, impact fees can be reduced or eliminated to create the necessary incentives for developers. Municipalities can offer appropriate credits or reductions in impact fees for development that achieves certain public goals (infill, redevelopment, density, location, mixed use, etc.) or creates a desired public benefit (such as providing needed amenities or services that would not be provided without the incentive).

Setting Standards for Growth

What important characteristics and qualities of your community are threatened by growth? There are dozens of possible answers that might include environmental quality, aesthetic qualities, open space, historic neighborhoods, traffic levels, and so forth. Hence, there are dozens of possible community standards to establish to protect your community from undesirable impacts of growth. By setting strict standards, the community is saying "we are not willing to sacrifice our clean water, clean air, or abundant natural resources to growth."

Threshold standards and *performance standards* are two forms of growth standards. An *environmental threshold standard* might require that water quality be maintained at or above current levels for all local streams, rivers, lakes, and aquifers. In order to comply, a new industry or development must demonstrate that it will not lower water quality.

In other words, no net increase in pollution emissions to local water ways would be allowed. A *quality-of-life threshold standard* might use a system of community benchmarks (based on indicators) to protect and improve local livability and other valued characteristics (see the Lake Oswego case study). Threshold standards represent a relatively new and promising frontier for growth management. They have the potential to protect community health and quality of life in fundamental ways and to exert a strong influence over how future growth occurs.

Growth standards can protect important qualities in your community in the following areas:

- environmental quality standards (air quality, surface, and ground water quality);

- maximum pollution emission levels (on a per capita or per employee basis);

- amenity standards (parkland, open space, recreation facilities, scenic vistas);

- community service standards (school, library capacity, police and fire protection);

- efficient resource usage requirements (land, water, power consumption);

- resource land preservation requirements (no net loss of farmland, wetlands);

- hazardous chemical usage restrictions;

- affordable housing requirements;

- historic and cultural resource preservation; and

- transportation system standards (congestion levels, travel times, access to alternative transportation).

To illustrate the application of a threshold standard, take the example of traffic congestion. Assuming that traffic levels are already high enough, the standard (or threshold) might be set at the current level of congestion. To establish what the current level of congestion is, hourly traffic volumes are measured on a selected group of representative streets over 24-hour periods. The same measurements can be repeated in the future to determine whether the standard is being maintained. The standard would require that a proposed new development demonstrate that it would not increase overall congestion levels.

There are various ways a development could be approved under

CASE STUDY: LAKE OSWEGO, OREGON — A COMMUNITY WITH STANDARDS

The City of Lake Oswego is located on the southern edge of Portland's city limits. It is bounded on the east by the Willamette River and on the west by the I-5 Freeway. To the south is the rural area of Stafford. The city grew from 19,400 to 33,145 people between 1975 and 1995. Most residents feel that the size of the city has already grown as much as it should (in terms of land area) and their focus is on protecting the quality of life enjoyed by current residents.

However, growth in the Portland area caused Metro, the regional planning organization, to plan for expansion of the region's urban growth boundary. In October, 1997 the Metro Council designated 2,056 acres in the rural Stafford area south of Lake Oswego as an urban reserve area. The urban reserve is intended to accommodate future expansion of Lake Oswego.

Anticipating this decision, the city worked for more than a year to craft an explicit growth policy that would protect the community from the likely impacts of this future growth. The city council and planning commission carefully deliberated on the proposed growth policy. They conducted surveys, held hearings, and sought extensive public involvement.

The resulting growth management policy received strong public support and was adopted by the city council on January 6, 1998 as a set of amendments to the city's comprehensive plan. Goal 14 of the plan (dealing with urbanization) was changed to read: *Lake Oswego shall ensure that the rate, amount, type, location, and cost of population growth and development within or outside of the Urban Services Boundary will not diminish the quality of life the City has presently attained.*

Quality of life is determined through a set of quality-of-life indicators that the city had already begun to create. These indicators are to be incorporated into development regulations as criteria for determining impacts of future development on the community. The city also adopted a policy of requiring that new development pay the full cost of extending urban services to that development.

this standard. A developer might choose to fund transportation system improvements that would reduce congestion enough to allow the additional demand created by the new project. Or, a developer might create an alternative transportation program for employees and customers. Also the developer could support public transit, create incentives to carpool, or reduce the existing demand in some other way.

Standards related to the relative capacity of public infrastructure are often called "level of service" or "LOS" standards. Many communities have already set a LOS standard for certain kinds of infrastructure

— typically roads. Unfortunately, the LOS for individual roadways may not be very useful as a growth standard because they continue to allow a decline in overall system performance. Commonly used road standards are based on an "A" through "F" rating for the number of vehicles per hour that can be accommodated. A LOS of "D" is often selected as lowest acceptable level for roads throughout the community. The problem with this system is that it allows all the roads that currently have better conditions (A–C) to degrade until they reach the unacceptable level of "D."

As mentioned in Chapter 4, Professor Paul Templet proposed standards for recruiting new industries based on the amount of chemical emissions per new job.[8] This kind of standard emphasizes two public goals: reducing pollution and increasing jobs. Templet found that states with lower emissions (per job) had higher employment. He suggested a similar standard for energy use per job.

Performance standards (and performance zoning) are other forms of growth standards used successfully to control the quality and character of development. Performance standards may specify aesthetic criteria, landscaping, affordability, proximity to urban services, amount of open space, and other characteristics of development. Some good examples of performance standards can be found in Chula Vista and Livermore, California and Breckenridge and Boulder, Colorado. These measures can be combined with a point or merit review system to focus new development on achieving community goals.

Growth Rate Limits

A growth rate limit caps the amount of new development that can take place each year to a level that the community considers to be acceptable. This could be a one-percent per year cap in the growth rate of the number of housing units or total commercial floor area. Building permits are then capped at these levels. The City of Petaluma is one of several cities that has successfully used rate caps for many years.

1972 saw the first adoption of growth limits in two American cities: Petaluma, California and Boca Raton, Florida. The Boca Raton limits were soon struck down by the courts because they were not based on sound planning and a clear policy rationale. However, Petaluma's 500-dwelling-units per year cap withstood legal challenges by homebuilders and is still in effect today. One possible reason for Petaluma's success is that the residential development cap is set quite high for a relatively small city. When originally enacted, it was equivalent to a five-percent per year growth rate. In recent years, building permit applications have been below the cap.

Rate caps have the interesting potential of creating competition among prospective developments for the limited allotments of construction permits. The cities of Boulder and Aspen, Colorado and Petaluma and Livermore, California have all taken advantage of this potential to foster better developments. They established criteria for ranking development proposals in terms of their desirability. Projects were ranked by a point system. A residential project, for example, would gain points by having a certain percentage of low- and moderate-income housing. Points would be awarded for architectural and site design quality, and for providing various needed public amenities such as bike paths, parkland, or open space. Smaller projects (defined as one-to-ten housing units, depending on the city) were exempt from the allocation system.

Livermore reviews its growth rate limit every three years to set a new annual limit between the 1.5 percent and 3.5 percent range allowed in the city's general plan. Proposed housing projects are ranked and selected based on a set of evaluation criteria. These include siting and layout, open space, landscaping, architectural design, energy efficiency, facility contributions (bike trails, infrastructure), innovations, and suitability of location.

Capping Ultimate City Size

Boulder, Colorado is one of a handful of communities that have decided to take steps to limit their ultimate size. Boulder is using its zoning regulations and the limited land supply within the current city boundaries as a means of controlling the ultimate "buildout" of the city. The density limits for residential housing and commercial floor space specified in the current zoning will indirectly result in population size limits. Boulder has recognized that job creation is a major factor in causing growth. For this reason the city has purchased some private commercial land to prevent it from being developed and has downzoned other commercial land. As described in the following case study, Boulder continues to be an innovative leader and model community for successfully controlling growth.

Adequate Public Facility Requirements

In countless cases, rapid growth has caused the demand for public

CASE STUDY: BOULDER, COLORADO — LEADING BY EXAMPLE

Located where the western edge of the Great Plains meets the Front Range of the Rocky Mountains, Boulder (population 93,000) enjoys a beautiful natural setting. The University of Colorado contributes cultural and intellectual diversity. These amenities, combined with a strong economy, caused Boulder to experience rapid growth in the two decades between 1950 and 1970, averaging about six percent per year. (At this rate of growth, a city's population doubles every 11.5 years!) By the late 1960s, residents had become keenly aware of the problems associated with growth.

In 1967, Boulder voters approved one of the nation's first locally funded greenbelt systems. They used a local sales tax increase of 0.4 percent to finance open space land acquisition. As of 1998, Boulder had raised $116 million and acquired 33,000 acres of greenways and mountain parks. The greenbelt system serves as a natural growth boundary, defining the limits of the city with open space and parkland. This natural boundary helps to block urban sprawl and "leapfrog" development. The greenbelt has also helped protect the quality of life in Boulder as the city has grown. It is said that more people use the greenbelt system each year than visit nearby Rocky Mountain National Park. As an added measure, Boulder established a building height limitation of 55 feet in 1971 to preserve the view of the Rockies. The city and surrounding county have cooperated on planning and growth-management policies and jointly adopted the Boulder Valley Comprehensive Plan. A city-county study in 1970 showed the area's population doubling in 20 years to 140,000. This projection alarmed many residents and prompted discussions about optimum population size. A public opinion survey found that more than 70 percent of respondents favored population stabilization near the 100,000 level.

In November, 1971 Boulder citizens set another first when they placed an initiative on the ballot to create a charter amendment setting a maximum population limit for the city. Voters narrowly defeated the initiative. The defeat may have been partly due to an alternative referendum placed on the same ballot by the city council. This second referendum was approved by 70 percent of voters and directed local government to "take all steps necessary to hold the rate of growth in the Boulder Valley to a level substantially below that experienced in the 1960s." This important decision has led to a number of experimental growth-management policies that are still being fine-tuned today.

In 1976, Boulder adopted residential growth limits (four years after similar limits were adopted in Petaluma, California). These limits initially capped the number of new dwelling units at 450 per year to keep the annual growth rate at 1.5 to two percent. (In previous years, the annual growth rate had averaged above three percent.) This plan helped revitalize the downtown, because 175 of the 450 permits were earmarked for the city center. Small projects (fewer than four units) on existing lots were exempted from the dwelling unit limits. The growth rate cap was lowered to one percent per year in 1995, and has remained at that level.

Originally, the residential permit caps were accompanied by a merit review system that was intended to help select the best development projects for approval (these were also based on Petaluma's model). A detailed point system was developed that awarded permits based on such criteria as availability of urban services, affordability, and energy efficiency. Projects that created low-and moderate-income housing (for rent or sale) received the most points. While the affordable housing incentive worked very well, the merit system was found to be too bureaucratic and was abandoned in 1981. The current system gives each applicant a proportionate share of the available building permits.

More recently, the city has sought to limit the rate of commercial development. For the past 15 years, the rate of job growth has exceeded population growth. Between 1980 and 1995, the population increased by 18,980 while the number of jobs grew by 27,000. While the residential growth controls had slowed population growth, they had done little to curb commercial development. Boulder's job growth has also contributed to the population growth of surrounding towns. This, in turn, caused increased traffic congestion in Boulder and resulted in over-use problems for city facilities and amenities.

As part of a city-wide visioning process, city planners evaluated various scenarios for the ultimate "buildout" of the city by the year 2020. They determined that their problems could get much worse before the city reached the end of its commercial land supply. The city council acted in September 1997 to reduce the potential number of new jobs the city could accommodate. Known as the "Comprehensive Rezoning Proposal," the program will reduce the ultimate number of new jobs at buildout by 15,000 to 20,000 through:

- purchasing commercially zoned land to prevent commercial development;
- rezoning industrial or commercial land to residential use; and
- changing zoning regulations to reduce the allowed size and density of new developments (downzoning).

As part of this program of limiting employment growth, the city recently bought several parcels of vacant industrial land, including 165 acres owned by IBM. New zoning regulations were adopted to limit commercial and industrial building sizes. Approximately one-third of the city was rezoned, including all industrial land.

A common criticism of Boulder's growth rate cap is that it has caused high housing prices. While Boulder's housing is expensive, it is not clear that the city's growth controls are the cause. Housing prices were high before any growth management programs were ever enacted. According to former-city planning director Bill Lamont, the rapid growth of the 1960s had already inflated housing prices and forced some lower-income people out of the city before the growth controls were implemented. Also, housing prices remained the same relative to those in nearby Denver both before and after the growth controls were implemented. (Boulder remained about 10-15 percent more expensive than Denver.)

When the annual growth rate cap was lowered to one percent in 1995, the city council also acted to create a larger share of affordable housing. New housing is allocated according to the following formula: 25 percent to market demand, 55 percent to affordable housing (based on size and other criteria) and 20 percent to permanently affordable housing maintained through deed restrictions. This housing allocation is combined with other programs such as a housing trust fund that uses an excise tax on new construction to subsidize low-income housing.

Colorado's Front Range communities are facing such extraordinary growth pressure that former governor Richard Lamm referred to the area in 1997 as the "Los Angeles of the Rockies."[9] In spite of this pressure, Boulder has managed to protect its quality of life and preserve its unique character by recognizing limits to growth and adopting responsible policies that are consistent with those limits.

facilities to outstrip the ability of communities to provide them. Classrooms become overcrowded and sewage plants overflow. Residents are faced with the choices of raising taxes, cutting services, or continuing to live with inadequate facilities.

Adequate public facilities requirements (also known as *concurrency requirements*) are intended to ensure that public facilities are in place as new development occurs. Such requirements seek to protect existing residents from declining levels of service, overloaded facilities, and increasing debt resulting from the demands of growth.

Florida and Washington have state statutes requiring concurrency. In order for a development to be approved, there must be adequate school, sewer, road, and water capacity in place at the time the project is completed. If a community is unable to afford the new facilities, a developer may be required to pay for them in order to obtain construction permits.

Figure 6-5
Boulder, Colorado's Greenbelt System

Boulder's greenbelt is the pride of the city (shown as shaded area in this map). It comprises 33,000 acres of publically owned parks and open space — twice the area of the city. The greenbelt is a physical boundary that acts to limit growth of the city. But it also attracts people who appreciate the beauty and access to nature it provides.

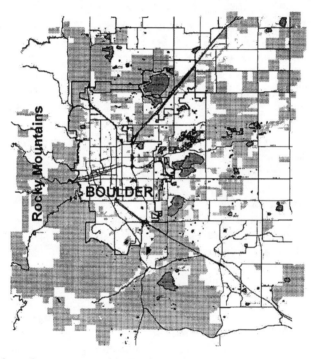

Source: Base map courtesy of the City of Boulder Open Space and Planning GIS Labs.
Reprinted with permission.

Urban Growth Boundaries and Greenbelts

An urban growth boundary (UGB) is a physical or legal boundary to the urbanized area of a city. Outside the UGB the land is considered rural and uses are limited to farming, forestry, and other non-urban purposes. A UGB can be very effective in controlling urban sprawl, but requires the cooperation of governments on both sides of the boundary — the city and the county. Cities in Oregon have considerable experience with

UGBs, since they have been a part of the statewide planning program for 25 years. The results have been mostly positive: a more orderly development of urban areas, lower costs to provide urban services, and protection of rural lands. By making rural land off limits to urban development, the level of land speculation is reduced. This makes farm and forest land more affordable and the business of farming and forestry more profitable.

John Fregonese, former chief planner at Metro, Portland, Oregon area's regional government, has estimated that about 20 U.S. cities will soon follow Portland's lead and establish urban growth boundaries as they realize they are rapidly "using up the one thing that nobody is making more of, and that's land." But Oregon's UGBs are not set in concrete. They can be expanded as part of a comprehensive plan amendment. More permanent boundaries can be created by establishing greenbelts of protected, undeveloped land. Boulder, Colorado used a greenbelt park system to define the limits of the city, along with some help from the Rocky Mountains. (Some methods for creating greenbelts are described in "Protecting Undeveloped Land," later in this chapter.

Annexation Restrictions

Annexation is the process through which municipalities expand their boundaries to include land outside the incorporated city limits. Developers often seek annexations in order to gain access to the urban services provided by the city. Expanding these services can result in a net burden on the city's taxpayers.

Policies restricting annexations can help ensure that development is compatible with the city and is fiscally balanced. Requiring a fiscal (or taxpayer) impact analysis is one approach. The impact on schools, transportation systems, and other facilities and services can be evaluated to identify potential costs or problems. Various techniques have been used to make local governments more accountable to the public in the annexation decisions. Some communities require that all annexations be put to a public vote. Others require a supermajority approval by the city council.

Downzoning

Zoning defines the kind of uses and development that can take place on land. Usually the zoning will set an upper limit to the allowable density. *Downzoning* reduces the allowed density. For example, land zoned to allow up to ten houses per acre might be downzoned to allow a maximum of five houses per acre. Downzoning has been widely used to lower the amount of growth that can legally be accommodated by a given land area. Alternatively, by raising this density limit (upzoning), more growth can be accommodated. In order to protect themselves from the negative impacts that can result from this additional growth, some cities require that upzonings be approved by a supermajority of the city council or that they be referred to voters.

Design Review/Public Review Process

A *design review process* is often used by communities seeking to improve the quality of development and to avoid unnecessary conflicts and negative impacts. A planning commission or design review board is used to evaluate proposed developments. Projects are evaluated based on an established set of criteria. Public notification and a public hearing should be part of the review process. Project evaluation criteria include landscaping, aesthetics, compatibility with the neighborhood, noise or other impacts on neighbors, traffic flows, and so forth. A design review process can also include a point or rating system where projects are approved only if they earn a certain threshold rating.

Without a public review process, citizens often have little control over individual developments, even if they will be severely impacted by them. Typically, a development proposal will be reviewed and approved by the city or county planning department, as long as the proposal meets the minimum requirements of the local zoning and land use code. But development codes cannot anticipate all the possible conflicts and impacts that future development might create. For large projects, creating a *public review process* may be the solution.

In the late 1980s, Washington, D.C. saw its biggest boom in commercial real estate in more than 30 years. Large office buildings, hotels, and retail outlets sprang up in what had been relatively quiet, older residential neighborhoods. The impacts were sometimes devastating to the neighborhood. Residents saw their on-street parking disappear and found that bumper-to bumper-rush hour traffic suddenly began at their front door. Unfortunately, there was little they could do except write angry letters to elected officials.

When a 400,000-square-foot office/retail complex began construction on Wisconsin Avenue near Tenley Circle, neighbors were alarmed at the scale and potential impact of the project. When they learned that the developers planned to pave part of the neighborhood's popular public park, many were outraged. Several neighbors were arrested in the park for blocking bulldozers with their bodies. (Ironically, they were each required to perform 100 hours of public service.) The neighbors organized into the Tenleytown and Cleveland

> **PUBLIC INVOLVEMENT?**
>
> *There are two stages to the public policy process: too early to tell, and too late to do anything about it.*
>
> — Anonymous

Park Emergency Committee. They raised funds, hired lawyers, sued the developer, and lobbied the mayor. As a result of this action, Mayor Marion Barry created a large tract review process that gave local neighborhood associations a 45-day public comment period before building permits were issued for all large projects of 50,000 square feet or more in size. Because neighborhood associations have an official advisory role in D.C. government, the city planning director is required to give their recommendations "great weight." If the neighborhood association strongly opposes a proposed development, the planning director will hold up the project approval until the issues are adequately resolved. Citizens are effectively empowered, through this process, to influence development in their own neighborhood before it becomes a "done deal."

Although the Wisconsin Avenue development went ahead and was completed, the tenor of subsequent development changed considerably after large tract review was implemented. Developers now present plans to the neighborhood associations as soon as they can to see if there will be any objections. This review process has resulted in many design improvements, has reduced negative impacts from development, and has generated long-term benefits for the neighborhoods and the city as a whole.

Community Impact Statements

Even with a good public review process like the one in Washington, D.C., there is often a lack of critical information by which to make informed decisions about the possible impacts of a particular development. In the case of some large developments, the impacts can affect the whole community. A community impact statement (CIS) is a means of evaluating these impacts and informing the public *before* developments are approved.

Most major cities require that a traffic impact study be conducted for large projects to determine what kinds of transportation system improvements are likely to be needed. The city may then negotiate with the developer to fund these improvements. A CIS evaluates a broader range of impacts that would include environmental, fiscal, and other elements. It might also include an explanation for why the project is needed and a market analysis showing the demand for a particular development.

In Lawrence Township, New Jersey, a CIS must be performed for all major subdivisions of ten or more lots or other major developments exceeding 50,000 square feet of floor space. According to Land Use Ordinance Section 813 and 814, the CIS must state why the application is in the public interest and include the following impact elements:

- Population: The number of people the project would add to the municipal population by age group.

- Schools: Expected increase in the number of students and the ability of the existing public school facilities to accommodate them over a ten-year period.

- Public Facilities: Availability of existing facilities to serve the proposed development, including water, sewage, recreation, libraries, and senior services.

- Public Services: Requirements for police protection, fire protection, solid waste disposal, and street maintenance services.

- Traffic: Analysis of the road network within and surrounding the proposed development.

- Financial: Analysis of both the revenues and costs anticipated from the project. Financial impacts are evaluated for the municipality, the school system, and the county.

According to Robert Minutoli, the township's director of Planning and Redevelopment, the CIS system has been in place for more than ten years and has worked well. Major developments are also required to submit an Environmental Impact Statement (EIS).

Environmental Impact Statements

Like the CIS, an EIS is a means of obtaining information about the environmental consequences of a development proposal before it is approved. The landmark U.S. National Environmental Policy Act (NEPA), enacted in 1970, created the requirement for an EIS for actions

IN THE WORDS OF **NEPA** ...

The Congress, recognizing the profound impact of man's activity on the interrelations of all components of the natural environment, particularly the profound influences of population growth, high-density urbanization, industrial expansion, resource exploitation, and new and expanding technological advances, and recognizing further the critical importance of restoring and maintaining environmental quality to the overall welfare and development of man, declares that it is the continuing policy of the Federal Government, in cooperation with State and local governments, and other concerned public and private organizations, to use all practicable means and measures, including financial and technical assistance, in a manner calculated to foster and promote the general welfare, to create and maintain conditions under which man and nature can exist in productive harmony, and fulfill the social, economic, and other requirements of present and future generations of Americans.[10]

— *U.S. National Environmental Policy Act of 1970* (Section 101)

undertaken, sponsored, and, in some cases, permitted by the federal government. The act requires all federal agencies to conduct an EIS for any action that may be defined as a "major federal action" that may involve a "significant impact on the natural environment." In the EIS the agency considers all environmental impacts of a given action, as well as the alternative actions and measures that may mitigate such impacts.

A number of state governments have emulated the NEPA with acts that apply to state-permitted or funded projects. The California Environmental Quality Act (CEQA) and the Minnesota Environmental Rights Act (MERA) are examples. CEQA applies to local government actions when they involve the enactment of zoning ordinances, conditional use permits, or subdivision maps.

Lawrence Township, New Jersey requires an EIS for all major land developments. The township's EIS is a comprehensive analysis that includes: a site description and inventory (soils, topography, geology, vegetation, wildlife, surface water, subsurface water, cultural resources, historic resources, etc.); an area and regional description (surrounding land uses, development, infrastructure, drainage, etc.); and environmental performance controls (measures to minimize on- and off-site impacts); and environmental impacts (flooding, water quality, noise, vegetation, wildlife, energy consumption, aesthetic effects, etc.).

The EIS ordinance stresses flexibility in the process due to variations in the nature of projects. The EIS is reviewed by the local Zoning Board and the development is not approved unless the Board finds that it:

- will not result in appreciable harmful effects to the environment;
- has been designed and conceived with a view toward the protection of regional resources; and
- will not place a disproportionate or excessive demand upon the total resources available for such proposal and for any future proposals.

Tax and Economic Incentives

The land development business relies heavily on economic decision-making. Therefore, it makes sense to influence development through economic incentives and disincentives. Taxes that increase the cost of development are likely to moderate the rate of growth. The *real estate transfer tax* is a widely used municipal revenue source that taxes the property sale based on a fixed percentage of the price. Like a sales tax, the real estate transfer tax might be set at one or two percent of the sale price. The tax is collected from the buyer or seller (or both) at the time of sale.

A local *land gains tax* on land value can capture some of the increase in property values that are created by the community. A land gains tax is used in several European countries and by the states of Connecticut and Vermont. A 1987 survey of growth management strategies identified 22 communities in the U.S. with land gains taxes.[11] In Vermont, rapid property turnover and high rates of gain are taxed at the highest rate of 80 percent, while profits on land owned for five years are taxed at ten percent. Land owned for more than six years has no tax on the gain. Both the transfer tax and the land gains tax tend to discourage land speculation.

A *construction tax* is charged on the value of new construction. The tax is collected at the time the building permits are issued. A construction tax can temper the pace of development while also providing a source of funds for planning and other growth-related expenses.

A *land tax* can be used in urban areas to encourage density and discourage sprawl. By taxing land rather than buildings, there is an incentive to develop each parcel of urban land to its fullest potential.

The opposite approach can be used outside urban areas to discourage rural or sprawling development (see "Conservation Tax Incentives" in the next section).

Growth Moratoria

Growth moratoria are most commonly used when there is inadequate capacity in one or more basic public facilities, such as sewage treatment, water supply, road capacity, or schools. They are typically achieved by ceasing to issue building permits for new construction. The moratorium may stay in place until the problem is resolved, which can sometimes take years (see Jacksonville case study).

Moratoria run up against one of the U.S. Constitution's basic liberties: the right to travel (or live where you want). We can't create "walls" around our communities that prevent people and goods from coming and going. Courts support temporary moratoria as long as the local government is seeking solutions to the problems that caused it to be enacted. It is unclear whether there are circumstances under which the courts would uphold a permanent moratorium.

Other Possible Growth Controls

Because growth controls are still in the experimental stages, there are many possible approaches yet to be tested by a local government. Five additional public policies that have the potential to moderate growth in a socially responsible manner are described below: infrastructure spending restrictions; limiting speculative development; consumption limits; carrying capacity limits; and ecological footprints.

Infrastructure Spending Restrictions. In 1997, Oregon governor John Kitzhaber became concerned about the deteriorating condition of the state's roads. He threatened to stop construction of new roads until the state legislature developed a means of funding maintenance of existing roads. This action was based on prudent fiscal policy: We should not be building new facilities when we can't afford to maintain the ones we already have. Unfortunately many municipal governments have precisely the opposite approach — they give top priority to growth-related infrastructure and new capital projects, even when the roof is leaking at City Hall. An explicit policy on infrastructure spending would prioritize both the maintenance and operation of all existing facilities before investing in new or expanded facilities. If your community is growing rapidly but can't afford to maintain public buildings or provide basic services, this may be the approach to use.

CASE STUDY: SIX-YEAR CONSTRUCTION MORATORIUM IN JACKSONVILLE, OREGON

The small historic town of Jacksonville (still only about 2000 people) lacked an adequate water supply to serve new development. Water pressure was quite low for the existing community and fire protection became an issue. The cost of developing a new water source was extremely high ($5.5 million) and the city lacked the necessary funds. The city council enacted a development moratorium in September 1990. The moratorium faced a court challenge, but held up under Oregon's limited moratorium statute. Unable to resolve funding problems, the moratorium was extended every six months. The city hired a new planner who was finally able to convince local residents that they should shoulder the debt for a new water system. The moratorium was lifted in April, 1996. Approximately 90 new dwelling units are currently planned.

It is interesting to note that Jacksonville's economy did not go into a recession during this extended moratorium, as some economists might have predicted. Instead, the town remained prosperous, in spite of the complete ban on development. The author visited the town shortly after the moratorium was lifted and found that commerce appeared to be doing extremely well. Restaurants and hotels were charging some of the highest rates in the state and doing a brisk business.

Limiting Speculative Development. In the late 1980s the commercial real estate market in many U.S. cities was growing so rapidly that banks were readily financing speculative development projects (projects without known tenants or buyers) with little regard for market demand. But the construction frenzy caused the office space market to overbuild. At one point the Washington, D.C. area had enough excess office space to meet the anticipated demand for the next ten years. The market collapsed, leaving many developers bankrupt and forcing banks to foreclose on empty buildings. U.S. taxpayers ended up paying the bill for much of this reckless speculation when hundreds of savings and loan institutions went under. The total cost to taxpayers of the savings and loan bailout by the federal government was $215 billion (1990 dollars).

This led to tougher lending policies requiring that 30-50 percent or more of the proposed office space have a rental contract before financing would be approved. Communities may be able to use this same approach to temper the enthusiasm of speculative development with market realities. For example, a requirement that a minimum percentage of the proposed development be pre-leased or pre-sold before building permits are issued, assures that there is some level of market demand for the project. An independent market analysis could also be required as part of the approval process.

Consumption Limits. In order to minimize land and resource consumption, certain limits are established. One approach that has been used is the maximum residential lot size. For example, by setting the maximum lot size at 10,000 square feet, a community is ensuring that the existing land supply is not consumed quickly with large lots. It may be possible to expand this type of policy to include maximum house sizes and other development characteristics that would tend to reduce resource consumption. *Minimum densities* are another means of accommodating growth with less land consumption. (This is the opposite approach to *downzoning,* mentioned earlier). If a particular residential zone allows densities of up to eight houses per acre, a minimum density standard might require that this land be developed with at least six houses per acre. This helps assure that land is not consumed in an inefficient manner. Some communities have set goals that new construction will occur at 80 percent or more of the allowed density. In Portland, Oregon, the Metro regional government set a density goal of ten dwelling units per acre of developable residentially zoned land. While this goal has been widely supported as a means of preventing sprawl, it is facing opposition from some residents who feel that the character and quality of their neighborhoods is threatened by higher density.

Carrying Capacity Limits. Carrying capacity reflects the ability of the environment to support a given species of plant or animal based on limiting factors such as water, nutrients, forage, and so forth. This biological concept has more recently been applied to human settlement. In this context, the carrying capacity is the maximum number of people that a given land area can sustain over the long term. In some places such as deserts and islands, water is the limiting factor. In other places it may be less clear what the actual limits are. Part of the uncertainty is due to constantly changing technology that has the potential to overcome some limiting factors. It may also be difficult to set practical boundaries for the land area of a particular human settlement because interstate and international trade tends to expand the realm of influence of most communities. However, in many areas of North America the levels of groundwater have been steadily declining as water is withdrawn faster than it is being recharged. These water demands have already exceeded regional carrying capacity.

Ecological Footprint. North American cities draw their resources from areas far beyond the city limits. How can we gauge the true environmental impact of the petroleum we import from Saudi Arabia and fruit from Chile? Mathis Wackernagel and William Rees developed a methodology for calculating the effective land area required to supply this level of consumption — the "ecological footprint."[12] An ecological footprint measures our consumption of food, housing, transportation, consumer goods, and services and then calculates the equivalent amount of land area required to provide them. While this concept has not yet resulted in policies for controlling urban growth, it can play an educational role by creating awareness of population, consumption, and growth issues.

PRESERVING UNDEVELOPED LAND

Public Land Acquisition, Conservation Easements, Purchasing Development Rights

Considering the high public costs associated with land development (see Chapter 5), public acquisition of land for conservation or other purposes can often *save local taxpayers money*. As surprising as it may sound, this is not news. A 1968 study of Closter, New Jersey found the cost of acquiring 80 acres of land to be less than the tax deficit that would result if the land were developed with 160 houses.[13] A 1970 study for the city of Palo Alto, California found that it was considerably cheaper for the city to purchase open land in its foothills rather than allowing it to be developed.[14]

More recently, a 1991 study found that the town of Yarmouth, Maine would incur a cost of $140,000 annually if a certain parcel of land were developed.[15] By purchasing the land the town's annual cost would be only $76,000, an annual savings of $64,000. The same study reports on a parcel in Huntsville, Alabama that, if developed, would have infrastructure costs of $5 million and annual service costs of $2,500 to $3,000 per acre. By contrast, acquisition would cost only $3.3 million and annual service cost were $75 per acre.

A 1996 study prepared for the Trust for Public Land found that the town of Londonderry, New Hampshire could save money by purchasing the *development rights* on 269 acres of land known as Mack Orchards.[16] The alternative of allowing the land to be developed with 87 houses would have cost the town $600,000 more over the 23-year study period assumed for the conservation bond repayment. By purchasing development rights and conserving the land in perpetuity,

CASE STUDY: LAND CONSERVATION SAVES MONEY IN PITTSFORD, NEW YORK

In 1996 the Town of Pittsford (population 25,000) decided to permanently preserve almost half of its remaining open space by purchasing the development rights to the land. Voters approved $10 million in municipal bonds to acquire the development rights to 1,200 acres of farmland, woods, wildlife habitat, and wetlands. According to the city, the reasons for taking this action were twofold: to save the most significant remaining resources in the community, which will preserve the character of Pittsford; and prevent development of the targeted farms which will help to stabilize the growth in taxes over the next twenty years.

A study by the city found that as a result of keeping this land undeveloped, the average Pittsford taxpayer would see a total net savings of $3,600 each over the next 20 years. This savings in school and property taxes results from avoiding the costs of providing urban facilities and services to developed land.

annual property taxes on existing homes in the town would be several dollars less than if it were developed. This conclusion was due, in part, to the fact that housing was found to cost the local government more in ongoing services than it generated in tax revenues.

Most cities routinely purchase land when needed for parks, roads, or stormwater drainage. However, if the goal is simply to maintain the undeveloped or natural character of an area, it may not be necessary to purchase the land. A *conservation easement* is a means of protecting land from development without the expense of fully acquiring the land. It might be used to keep land in a natural state or to keep actively farmed land from being further developed. It does not result in a change of ownership.

Purchasing development rights is a similar approach to the conservation easement. The local government buys the future development rights (or other usage rights) from the owners but allows continued ownership and use of the land for non-development purposes such as farming, recreation, or access. A permanent easement is recorded in the property deed and transfers with the land. According to the *New York Times*, in the 20 years since Suffolk County, New York began the first program to buy development rights from farmers, such buyouts have preserved 450,000 acres of farmland in 18 states.[17] Montgomery County, Maryland and King County, Washington are two examples of successful, large-scale land conservation using this method.

Transferrable Development Rights

To protect land from development in an area designated for conservation, the development rights are separated from the land and allowed to be transferred to another area that can better accommodate the development. These development rights can thereby be sold to compensate the owner of the land designated for conservation. To have value, the transferrable development rights (TDRs) must allow increased levels of development elsewhere that are not already permitted. This increased development can be a problem with TDRs, since there is often a good reason why higher densities are not already allowed in other areas.

One of the most successful TDR programs for natural area protection has preserved 10,000 acres of forest, farmland, and cedar swamp in the Pinelands National Reserve in New Jersey. Montgomery County, Maryland has a successful TDR program for farmland preservation.

Community Land Trusts

Private, non-profit land trusts are a popular and highly successful means of conserving land. They have been created to protect land from development, to preserve farmland, to create low-income housing, and for other purposes. The land trust simply acquires land and then puts it to the use for which the trust was created.

As tax-exempt charitable organizations, land trusts can acquire lands through charitable donations that may provide financial benefits to the grantor landowners who will derive tax savings from such transactions. The trust often recoups its investment in the land by selling the property to the local government at a lower price than the government would have had to pay.

According to The Land Trust Alliance, a national umbrella organization, land trusts have protected approximately four million acres of wetlands, wildlife habitat, ranches and farms, shorelines, forests, recreation land, and other property of ecological significance. The number of local land trusts has grown from 535 in 1985 to more than 1,100 in 1998. Land trusts are operating in every state of the U.S.

Public Land Banking

When a local government, or a specially created public entity, buys large areas of land and holds them for a future use, it is commonly referred to as land banking. A land bank gives the public more control over land use decisions. It can make the process of land development more orderly and can reduce land speculation. A land bank helps ensure that adequate land is available for parks, schools, and other municipal needs. Land banking requires a lot of money up front, but has the potential to save taxpayers money in the long run. The land that is acquired in a land bank can be leased for agricultural or other purposes. However, public land banking has not been widely used since the idea was introduced in the early 1970s.[18]

Open Space Requirements

Some communities have adopted requirements that all new development provide a certain amount of open space or undeveloped land. Adams County, Colorado requires a 20-25 percent land dedication for open space in residential developments. Pittsford, New York requires that 50 percent of the land in new developments be open space.

Conservation Tax Incentives

Tax incentives can be used to encourage landowners to protect their land in certain ways by setting lower property tax rates for farm, forest, or open space land. By lowering the tax on undeveloped land, there is less economic pressure for the owner to sell or develop the land. (The opposite technique of heavily taxing land, but not buildings can be used in developed urban areas to encourage greater density.) To discourage land speculation, some or all of the tax savings should be recovered by the community if the land is eventually developed.

Exclusive Agricultural Zoning

Farm and forest land can be maintained through restrictive zoning that limits other uses of the land. Zoning can protect rural lands from intensive development with large minimum lots sizes (such as 80 acres) and restrictions on parceling land into smaller lots.

GAINING PUBLIC SUPPORT FOR GROWTH CONTROLS

The implementation of any kind of growth management depends on having the necessary political support, or better yet, a public mandate to carry it through. You might be surprised to know that most people support growth management. But growth issues are often complex and confusing to the general public. Citizens need better information about growth impacts, future growth projections, and positive alternatives to more growth-as-usual.

Figure 6-6
Number of California Jurisdictions with Growth Measures

Type of Measure	Cities	Counties
Residential infrastructure requirements	112	17
Residential downzoning	106	15
Restrict permitted commercial/office building heights	100	12
Commercial/industrial infrastructure requirements	92	16
Urban limit line or greenbelt	56	23
Other, pending	47	7
Growth-management element of general plan	43	8
Housing permit limitations	43	7
Rezone commercial/industrial land to less intense use	40	5
Population growth caps	38	2
Other, enacted	32	2
Rezone residential land to less intense use	19	8
Require voter approval for upzoning	17	2
Commercial square footage limitations	13	1
Industrial square footage limitations	12	1
Require council supermajority for upzoning	10	1

Source: *Regional Growth ... Local Reaction.* The authors surveyed all of California's 443 jurisdictions and identified total of 907 different growth-management measures.[6]

A public opinion survey can serve as an indication of the public interest on a given issue. A good survey can be the basis for introducing new policies to control growth. A well-designed survey on growth attitudes should ask clear, simple, unbiased questions and allow a full range of responses. The following are examples of survey questions that are likely to yield meaningful results:

- How has recent growth affected you personally? Has the overall impact of growth been positive or negative?

- In the future, do you want to see more growth or less growth?

- In your opinion, what is the ideal population of your community? Is the ideal size larger, smaller, or about the same size as it is today?

A 1974 survey asking a similar question in Santa Barbara found that 83 percent expressed a preference for a same-sized or smaller city.[19] When asked about the preferred size of their neighborhood, 97 percent favored a same-sized or smaller neighborhood.

Support for growth management is likely to be strongest in high-growth areas where people are experiencing the impacts of growth — up close and personal. Public preference for growth-management crosses all demographic lines. Results are fairly consistent across age, income, gender, ethnicity, and education levels. The weakest support for growth management is likely to come from the wealthiest segment of the population and from members of the organized business community.

A 1996 survey conducted by the City of Eugene, Oregon polled residents on their preference for various growth-management options ranging from promoting growth to discouraging growth. The survey showed strong support for slowing growth by every cross section of the population except one — members of the Chamber of Commerce. This group favored the option that would actively promote growth. Aside from the Chamber members, the next weakest support for slowing growth came from those respondents with annual incomes above $100,000 (although a majority of this group also favored slowing growth).

Public opinion surveys such as the ones mentioned above are a valuable tool for gauging public support for growth management. By creating opportunities to consider the issues in more detail, by providing educational public forums, and by making quality information available, the support for slowing growth is likely to be even stronger.

THE NEW MILLENNIUM COMMUNITY

We have lived by the assumption that what was good for us would be good for the world. We have been wrong. We must change our lives, so that it will be possible to live by the contrary assumption that what is good for the world will be good for us. And that requires that we make the effort to know the world and to learn what is good for it. We must learn to cooperate in its processes, and to yield to its limits. But even more important, we must learn to acknowledge that the creation is full of mystery; we will never clearly understand it. We must abandon arrogance and stand in awe. We must recover the sense of the majesty of the creation, and the ability to be worshipful in its presence. For it is only on the condition of humility and reverence before the world that our species will be able to remain in it.

— Wendell Berry, *Recollected Essays 1965-1980*

Is today's lifestyle all you would want it to be? Do you have time to recreate, relax, and socialize? Is there convenient access to nature and the outdoors? Do you enjoy fresh air and clean water? Do you have the opportunity to garden and grow some of your own food if you want to? Is there a sense of community where you live? Is your neighborhood safe for your children to play in? Can you walk and bike conveniently and safely around your community if you choose to? Do you and your children feel optimistic and hopeful about the outlook for the future? Do you feel confident that your health and welfare will be protected by society should you fall into misfortune? Are you satisfied that your economy and society are fair and equitable?

If you answered no to any of these questions, you may see the potential for our new millennium community to be a better place for you and your children. I am not suggesting that people move to some new age community. Quite the opposite. I suggest that you not move at all. Stay put. Stop thinking about escaping to some better place over the next horizon. Make your community the kind of place it should be.

Citizens actively engaged in their communities will continue to be the strongest force for progressive change in the new millennium. There are many actions you can take to move your community in the direction of sustainability, but taking control of urban growth tops the list of priorities. A good place to start this transition is with a positive vision for an alternative to endless growth — a stable, sustainable community. What can this sustainable community offer you, your family, and your neighbors that your current community does not? If the sustainable community is to exist, it must be a healthier, happier, better place to live. What would make this sustainable community one *you* would want to live in?

It's quite hard to imagine a truly sustainable community existing in our current society. Our cities are so busy growing and are so dependent on imported energy and resources that it seems unlikely, if not impossible, for them to achieve sustainability. We can be sure, however, that our society will eventually recognize ecological limits and adopt sustainability principles, or it will perish. The great mystery of the new millennium is how and when this change will happen.

I believe the key to such a change is a shift in our values, which already seems to be underway. It has the potential of being a rapid, sweeping shift — the kind we might have thought impossible before it happened. We could not have forecasted the remarkable way society adapted to the energy crisis of the 1970s. Nor could we have foreseen such a rapid conclusion to the cold war and de-escalation of the nuclear threat. Or that the Internet would emerge as such a powerful tool for education, public involvement, and democracy. This shift in values that I anticipate is one of discovery and fulfillment, in which we find that the things we really want and need are very different than what we had thought previously.

But how can we have a clear notion of our real needs and wants when they are being distorted to such a degree by a continual barrage of commercial messages. Like the fish that bites on a fisherman's shiny lure, we are attracted to things that are glittery but not necessarily good for us. We go for fatty, processed food over fresh, wholesome foods. We drink a sugary soda instead of a glass of water. We choose the convenience and ease of driving a few blocks over the relaxing and healthy exercise of walking or biking. We choose an evening in front of the television, instead of meeting with friends.

These choices are, at first glance, what we want. The fish wants the shiny lure until it is too late and he has been caught. We opt for the 150 channels of television viewing, but find we are spending most of our free time sitting on a couch, staring at a video screen. A new appliance sounds like it will improve our life, but ends up taking up space and wasting our money. New fashions promise to make us look great, but what was wrong with last year's clothes that also promised to make us look great? Technology continually creates things we never knew we needed. How many of us were longing for fiber optics, high definition television, or digital video disks before they were invented?

We can waste a lot of our lives chasing after fish lures that offer us little substance. In the same way that the fish is tricked, we too are tricked. The fish would be best off sticking to a diet of live insects and swimming in the clean, cold mountain stream. Millions of years of evolution have adapted it to thrive in these conditions. Its defect was to be attracted to the hard, shiny metal of an artificial meal that mimics the real meal. As economist Herman Daly has said,

> "Whatever the public chooses is assumed to be in the public interest, and there is no distinction between what people of the present age of advertising *think* will make them whole and happy and what would *in fact* make them so."[1]

Our modern society has managed to all but isolate us from Nature, which was once our dearest friend. Children, who are fascinated by nature and love the outdoors, are weaned from it as quickly as possible. We go from air-conditioned homes to air-conditioned cars to air-conditioned offices without more than a puff or two of fresh air in between. Our neighbors rarely see us as we scoot our car deftly out of the garage, letting the door close automatically after us. We have banished dirt, cold, wet, discomfort, inconvenience, and delay from our day.

Let's assume that our values shift away from consumption and growth and towards simplicity and stability. We rebuild our bond with the natural world. We discover the neighborhood that we live in and meet the people next door for the first time. We discover a sense of place. We find that our community is not all it could be and we make changes. We re-prioritize our lives and find that we want to spend much more time with our families and good friends, even if we have to cut back work hours and reduce our incomes.

In spite of these changes, we find that occasionally the fish lure still attracts us. So we create incentives to encourage healthy, productive activities. We reward ourselves for doing what's best for us. We use green taxes to reduce consumption of resources and to minimize wastes. We replace income taxes with progressive consumption taxes. We eliminate the influence of unwanted commercial advertising altogether, relying instead on other information sources (such as Internet databases and search engines) to find all the products that aren't conveniently available through local merchants.

Amazingly, the entire economy starts to change. Like the circulatory system of our bodies, it quietly delivers the nutrients we need without dominating our lives. With the economy shifted from center stage, society rediscovers cultural, intellectual, and spiritual pursuits. We are entertained by life's richness and wonders.

This vision does not seem far-fetched to me. In fact, it appears to be just around the corner. All we have to do is decide to make the turn. We needn't make the turn right away, but the longer we wait the less likely the transition will be accomplished smoothly and painlessly.

WHAT IS A SUSTAINABLE COMMUNITY?

It's time we started planning our society and our communities as though we were going to be around for awhile, instead of only another ten or 20 years. Since our survival is clearly at stake, we must take the longer view in planning and decision-making. This is what *sustainable community planning* is all about. The concept of sustainability is one of extended time frames. A sustainable society is durable and has potential to continue into the distant future. A sustainable society does not impoverish future generations nor jeopardize their prospects by its current actions.

To be truly sustainable over the long term, the new millennium community must meet the basic sustainability criteria adapted from Herman Daly:[2] It will use renewable natural resources no faster than they can be replenished; it will use non-renewable resources like petroleum no faster than we can develop renewable substitutes like solar energy; and it will discharge wastes into the environment no faster than nature can absorb them. An additional criteria might be added that specifically includes protecting ecological integrity.

The best time frame for evaluating questions of sustainability is *forever*. By extending the time frame indefinitely, it is possible simplify the definition of sustainability: *A sustainable action, policy,or process is one that can be continued indefinitely without degrading the ecological integrity and life supporting capacity of the natural environment.*

This benchmark for sustainability provides a convenient and intuitive check for the many decisions we continually make about our lifestyles and our communities: If it can be continued forever, it is sustainable.

When we apply this test to urban growth, we easily see that our continued conversion of land to urban use is not sustainable. In fact, quantitative growth of any kind is not sustainable. Population growth is not sustainable. As we saw in Chapter 6, even if population growth occurs at the apparently slow rate of one percent per year, the population will double every 70 years and the consequences will eventually become impossible. Growth of our already high consumption levels is not sustainable. Albert Bartlett proposed a "First Law of Sustainability," summarized as: *Growth in population or consumption levels is not sustainable.*[3]

Qualitative growth, on the other hand, *is* sustainable. There is no limit to how much information, understanding, or enlightenment we can acquire. There is no limit to diversity, complexity, or variety. There is no limit to creativity, enterprise, or ambition. There is no limit to personal growth or achievement. A sustainable community can be a dynamic and evolving place. There is no limit to the richness of our lives in such a community.

Economist Herman Daly uses the example of the steady-state library to illustrate how there can be continual improvement without quantitative growth. The steady-state library does not increase in size and can accommodate only so many books. New books can be added at any time, as long as an equal number of books are removed. A new book will be added only if it is better than the book that is removed. In this way the library continually improves its selection.

THE SUSTAINABLE ECONOMY

Sustainability is an extremely tough standard to set for today's resource-gobbling, pollution-belching cities. Our economies are in high gear to achieve maximum output. Is it realistic to think a change to sustainable economies is possible?

We have continually sought both urban and economic growth in communities throughout North America. This growth has ceased only when economic conditions became so bad that it could not continue. The stigma of a non-growing community is that it is suffering from economic decline and hardship. This thinking is the result of a backwards association: If recessions cause communities to stop growing, then stable communities must also be recessionary. But until we *intentionally* create a stable community we will not know for sure what the real levels of economic well-being can be.

Daly has led economic thinking about the stable, or steady-state, economy for the past 30 years. He explains steady-state economics in terms of global constraints:

> The economy grows in physical scale, but the ecosystem does not. Therefore, as the economy grows it becomes larger in relation to the ecosystem. Standard economics does not ask how large the economy should be relative to the ecosystem. But that is the main question posed by steady-state economics ....

> It is important to be clear about what is not constant in a steady-state economy. Knowledge and technology are not held constant. Neither is the distribution of income nor the allocation of resources. The steady-state economy can develop qualitatively but does not grow in quantitative scale, just as planet Earth, of which the economy is a subsystem, develops without growing.[4]

Our economy is busily producing goods and services to satisfy what seems to be an unlimited consumer appetite. Studies show that our perceived needs are socially defined: the more our friends and neighbors have, the more we want. Needs are also defined in terms of what we currently have. Regardless of our current income levels, we believe we would be satisfied if we had just a little more income. The more we have, the more we want.

If there is no limit to our needs, then there is no point at which we will have enough. Our ever-growing levels of consumption may provide some temporary gratification but they do not lead to what people are really seeking: happiness. According to Alan Durning in his book, *How Much is Enough*, "The main determinants of happiness in life are not related to consumption at all — prominent among them are satisfaction with family life, especially marriage, followed by satisfaction

Figure 7-1   Buddhist Economics

A comparison of Buddhist and Western attitudes towards the economy.

	Buddhist	Western
Labor	Seek right livelihood in order to develop one's faculties and to contribute to society in a way that reflects well on oneself.	A disutility, to be eliminated (the employer wishes output without workers; the employee, income without work).
Leisure	Is complementary to work; both are necessary.	Leisure is preferable to work.
Technology	Tools are to help humans do creative work.	Technology is a means for abolishing human work.
Trade	A sign of local economic imbalance and failure.	A sign of economic progress.
Goal of Life	To perfect one's character through good work which nourishes the spirit.	To accumulate wealth to satisfy unlimited wants.
Unemployment	Is unacceptable; all who want jobs should have them; mothering is a socially-esteemed profession.	Is tolerable; one who is not employed is probably lazy; mothering is not socially useful work, since it is not paid.
Nature of Work	Should be simple, non-violent, sparing of resources, use local materials, and provide satisfaction.	Is energy-consuming, high pressure, competitive, anxiety-creating; often employs imported materials.
Quality of Life	Consumption is incidental to living; attachment to wealth interferes with satisfaction; one's role is to blend with the environment, to protect it and to revere life.	Consumption levels measure standard of living; nature is to be conquered and controlled; one should consume whatever comes to hand – one is a fool not to.
Material Goods	Should be simple, long-lasting, beautiful, unique, and as few as possible to live well.	Should be complex, mass-produced, cheaply made, short-lived, and as numerous as possible.

Source: *Ariadne's Thread: The Search for New Modes of Thinking.* Reprinted with permission from Mary E. Clark.[6]

with work, leisure to develop talents, and friendships." The key sources of happiness, then, can be identified as social relationships, work, and leisure — none of which depend on any level of consumption or degree of wealth. It is possible that our obsession with consumption actually detracts from our ability to be happy. By directing our energy and attention to superficial gratification, we are distracted from those pursuits that really make us happy.

> *"Our possessions are our sorrows."*
>
> — Buddhist expression

Rather than struggle to meet our unbounded perceptions of need, we must come to some understanding about how much is *sufficient.* Our economy can be deployed to provide sufficient goods and services to everyone, while discouraging excessive levels of consumption. As Daly has said: "Once we have replaced the basic premise of 'more is better' with the much sounder axiom that 'enough is best,' the social and technical problems of moving to a steady state become solvable, perhaps even trivial."[5]

Economist E. F. Schumacher said in his landmark book, *Small is Beautiful*:

> [The modern economist] is used to measuring the "standard of living" by the amount of annual consumption, assuming all the time that a man who consumes more is "better off" than a man who consumes less. A Buddhist economist would consider this approach excessively irrational: since consumption is merely a means to human well-being, the aim should be to obtain the maximum of well-being with the minimum of consumption.

Schumacher outlined an alternative view of the economy in what he termed *Buddhist economics*. Figure 7-1 contrasts Buddhist economics with Western economics.

TWELVE-STEPS TOWARDS A SUSTAINABLE COMMUNITY

There are straightforward, practical steps you can take right now to move your community toward greater sustainability. Most of these steps can be accomplished within a year or two. They are possible within our current legal framework and do not require overhauling the political or economic system. What's more, these steps make sense for all communities, not only to achieve greater sustainability, but because they simply lead to better communities. Each of the following 12 steps toward sustainable communities can be taken individually. However, together they form an integrated strategy that will generate a stream of valuable, long-term benefits.

1. **Build a positive vision.** A positive, shared, long-range vision for the future can provide the inspiration, motivation and direction to propel a community forward and encourage the various interest groups to work together with a common purpose. Developing a community vision requires broad participation and may involve extensive public input. Visions change and must be updated on a regular basis. (See example in Figure 7-2.)

2. *Improve citizen involvement.* Broad, open citizen involvement in public planning and policy-making respects and enhances our democratic process. Increased citizen involvement generates many benefits, including policies that better serve the broader public interest. Citizen involvement doesn't just happen. Local governments must actively engage citizens and create productive processes for meaningful involvement. Public hearings are just a small part of the venue for actively involving citizens. Others include public forums, town hall meetings, round-table sessions, televised broadcasts, surveys, speaker series, etc. It's difficult to overstate the importance of strong public involvement processes in achieving good governance. The desire for expediency and economy on the part of policy-makers can cause them to take costly short cuts with public involvement. Citizens who are empowered with opportunities for meaningful participation will tend to appreciate and support their government and not lead anti-government tax revolts.

3. *Provide economic opportunity and equity.* The basic economic needs of the entire community must be met without compromising the quality of the natural environment. Local economic development must be focused on the long-term welfare of existing residents. We should strive to distribute the benefits of the local economy broadly and equitably.

4. *Use land wisely.* Land is a finite resource with no substitute. Consequently, we should use land efficiently and intelligently and strive to keep the urban footprint as small

GETTING STARTED

Here are some things you can do now to get involved and help your community take charge of urban growth:

- Run for elected office.
- Serve on the planning commission or zoning board.
- Participate in your neighborhood organization.
- Volunteer for a citizen advisory committee to your local government.
- Join an organization. (If there are no organizations working for responsible growth and land use, try the League of Women Voters, your local Sierra Club chapter or form a new organization yourself.)
- Testify at public hearings.
- Call or write your council representative.
- Write a letter to the editor.
- Organize a meeting.
- Circulate a petition.
- Monitor the city council and local government.
- Keep a file of information about local growth and development.
- Request to be on city notification lists for land use changes and development applications.

as possible to minimize environmental impact. Comprehensive, long-range planning is an essential tool for wise land use. A commitment to comprehensive planning requires adequate funding to implement the initial plan and for ongoing updates every five years or so. A wise land use plan recognizes that rural land is not merely "future urbanizable land." A plan to permanently protect farmland, forests, and open space should be included.

5. *Provide better information.* Good decisions require good information, including natural resource inventories and status reports, growth forecasts, alternative scenarios, policy analysis, development impact analysis, etc. Disseminate information widely and make it readily accessible to everyone. Good government starts with an informed public — it's the cornerstone of democracy.

6. *Use indicators and benchmarks for progress.* Indicators are a tool for improving public policy and monitoring the status of a community and its environment. Benchmarks are goals that can be measured with indicators to help ensure that public policies lead to progress and long-term sustainability.

7. *Use full-cost accounting.* Acknowledge the full environmental, social, and economic costs of growth and development. Evaluate these costs in making policy decisions. Eliminate subsidies that distort markets and cause overdevelopment. Enact pay-as-you-grow policies.

8. *Think long range.* Consider the impact decisions will have far into the future. Extend long-range community planning horizons to 50 or 100 years (instead of ten or 20 years). Utilize computer modeling capabilities to evaluate the long-range consequences of current trends and compare alternatives.

9. *Encourage efficient resource use.* Set efficiency goals for energy, water, and other resource uses for all sectors: residential, commercial, industrial and transportation. Use incentives and regulations to minimize resource consumption and waste production and maximize re-use and recycling by businesses and households.

10. *Make neighborhoods walkable.* Safe, friendly, walkable neighborhoods designed to eliminate automobile dependence will be one of the most visible attributes of the sustainable community. Walking is the oldest and most reliable form of transportation. It has a proven track record dating back four million years that justifies its being treated as a major component of all local transportation plans. Create automobile-free zones and automobile-independent housing complexes where walkers and bicyclists enjoy the privilege of maximum access and convenience.

11. *Preserve unique features.* Preserve features of local and regional significance: valuable farmland, forests and open space, and unique natural, scenic, recreational, historic, or cultural resources. Treat these natural assets as priceless family heirlooms to be passed on to future generations.

**Figure 7-2
Vision Statement
Minnesota Sustainable Development Initiative[7]**

- We Minnesotans make commitments and choices to preserve the options future generations will need to secure the quality of life we now enjoy.

- We see sustainable development as a positive, fundamental change in the way we define social progress, do business, and protect the environment.

- We view the health of our natural environment, the strength of our community, and our economic security as interdependent.

- We maintain our quality of life through sustainable use of energy and natural resources, recognizing that population growth, resource consumption, and lifestyle choices determine the options we leave for future generations.

- Our communities are places where all citizens enjoy rich opportunities in education, employment, involvement, and appreciation of the environment.

- Our economy is healthy, diversified, globally competitive, and in harmony with Minnesota's ecosystems; it provides all citizens ample opportunity for a fulfilling life.

- Our natural environment is biologically and ecologically diverse and able to provide the resource benefits, products, and services needed for the indefinite future.

- We continually work to change our political and economic systems so that they consistently reward economically efficient, socially beneficia,l and environmentally sustainable behavior.

The Minnesota Sustainable Development Initiative is an impressive example of a statewide effort to reconcile economic goals with a desire to protect the environment. Launched by Governor Arne H. Carlson in 1993 and administered by the State Environmental Quality Board, the initiative involved 105 appointed business, environmental, and civic leaders. The principles of sustainable development are advanced through cooperative public/private discussions, research, and a statewide congress.

12. *Recognize physical limits to growth and consumption.*
Population size, resource consumption, land use, and pollution levels must be in balance with the complex environmental support system. Start by acknowledging that physical and practical limits do exist. Then, try to identify what these limits are in terms of desirable, optimal, or ideal conditions. This book provides many of the tools needed to achieve desired limits on urban growth.

CONCLUSION

The Catch 22 of Growth described in Chapter 4 is especially relevant when considering the potential advantages of stable communities. Unlike the growing community that can never get ahead of its employment and housing problems, a stable community can progress in all sorts of areas. If a community can prevent itself from being overrun by growth, it has the potential to provide good jobs and adequate housing for everyone. It has the opportunity to provide better government at a lower cost. The non-growing community could have ample parkland and open space, be surrounded by permanently rural lands, have a vital downtown, maintain high-quality schools, and preserve quiet neighborhoods and safe, pedestrian-friendly streets. What's more, its outlook for the future is bright — continued livability and high overall quality of life!

Of course, the more wonderful our stable, sustainable community becomes, the more people will want to move there and the greater the political pressure will be to relax or undo growth controls. The strategies for restricting and moderating growth described in Chapter 6 will go a long way toward fending off growth pressures. Ultimately, communities may need stronger support from state and federal legislatures and the courts to control their destinies over the long run. Right now, our society can do more to fully empower communities to make choices about whether or not to continue growing. We can explicitly authorize local governments to curtail growth when citizens demand it or when responsible policy requires it. This kind of authority can be granted in such a way that it clearly serves the greater public welfare and does not lead to abuse or discrimination. With society's permission to stop growing, local governments will find many new solutions for controlling growth.

If there has been one message of this book, it is that further growth is far more likely to be the problem than the solution for today's communities. Urban growth is not something to be sought after like a prize or a blessing. Instead, it is more like a parasite that saps the strength and will of our communities. It continually erodes economic, environmental, and social conditions, and prevents communities from achieving their aspirations. By taking control of growth in your community, you can shift the focus of its energies from how to accommodate more growth to how to become a better place to live. This will enable your community to achieve new heights for livability, sense of community, environmental quality, public services and amenities, participatory democracy, and much more.

CHAPTER NOTES

I. THE ENDANGERED LANDSCAPE

1. "Front Porch Forum: The Jury is In," *The Seattle Times*, October 19, 1997.
2. Meadows, Donella H., Dennis L. Meadows and Jorgen Randers, *Beyond the Limits*, (Post Mills, Vermont: Chelsea Green Publishing Company, 1992).
3. U.S. Department of Agriculture, *1992 National Resource Inventory*. www.nhq.nrcs.usda.gov/nrihigh.html.
4. Vitousek, P. M., P. R. Ehrlich, et al. "Human Appropriation of the Products of Photosynthesis," *Bioscience*, vol. 36 (1986) pp. 368–73.
5. Wilson, Edward O., *The Diversity of Life* (Cambridge, Massachusetts: Belknap Press of Harvard University Press: 1992).
6. Pimentel, David and Marcia Pimentel, *U.S. Food Production Threatened by Rapid Population Growth*, prepared for Carrying Capacity Network, Washington, D.C., October 30, 1997. www.envirolink.org/orgs/gaia-pc/Pimentel2.html.
7. Pimentel, D. and M. Giampietro, "U.S. Population Growth Threatens Irreplaceable Farmland," *CCN Clearinghouse Bulletin* (Washington, D.C.: Carrying Capacity Network, December 1994).
8. Leinberger, Christopher B., "Metropolitan Development Trends of the Late 1990s: Social and Environmental Implications" (1995) and *Planning and Zoning News* (January 1993) in *Land Use in America* (1996).
9. U.S. Federal Highway Administration, Nationwide Personal Transportation Survey (1990).
10. Wackernagel, Mathis and William Rees, *Our Ecological Footprint: Reducing Human Impact on the Earth* (Gabriola Island, B.C.: New Society Publishers, 1996).
11. Bartlett, Dr. Albert, Emeritus Physics Professor, University of Colorado, Boulder, personal correspondence.

2. MEET THE URBAN GROWTH MACHINE

1. Altshuler, Alan A and Jose A Gomez-Ibanez, *Regulation for Revenue: A Political Economy of Land Use Exactions* (Washington, D.C.: Brooking Institute; Cambridge, Massachusetts: Lincoln Institute of Land Policy, 1993). Authors are professors of public policy and planning at Harvard University with appointments at the Kennedy School of Government and the Graduate School of Design. Altshuler is also the Kennedy School's Academic Dean and Director of its Taubman Center for State and Local Government.

2. Molotch, Harvey, "The City as a Growth Machine: Toward a Political Economy of Place," *American Journal of Sociology*, vol. 82 (2) (1976) pp. 309-30. See also Logan, John R. and Harvey L. Molotch, *Urban Fortunes: The Political Economy of Place* (Berkeley: University of California Press, 1987).

3. Monfort, Kenneth, *The Denver Post*, 2 August 1989, p. 6B.

4. Huszar, Paul C. and David W. Seckler, "The Perverse Dynamics of Growth," *Change and Growth* (October 1975). The authors wrote this article as professors in the Department of Economics at Colorado State University.

5. Ibid.

6. Hardin, Garrett, "The Tragedy of the Commons", *Science*, vol. 162 (December 1968) pp. 1243–48.

7 Kerr, Andy, "Growth Not Good For (Most) Oregonians", *Oregon's Future* (spring 1997) p. 14.

8 A good example of a public advocate for land use can be found in the Township of West Orange, New Jersey. A full-time PA position was created in 1988. In 1996 the role was expanded to two positions: one for zoning decisions and one for other planning issues.

3. THE TWELVE BIG MYTHS OF GROWTH

1. Altshuler, Alan A. and Jose A. Gomez-Ibanez, *Regulation for Revenue: A Political Economy of Land Use Exactions* (Washington, D.C: Brooking Institute; Cambridge, Massachusetts: Lincoln Institute of Land Policy, 1993) p. 77.

2. Lamm, Richard D., "Local Growth: Focus of a Changing American Value", *Management and Control of Growth*, vol. III, chap. 16 (Urban Land Institute, 1975). See also Black, Thomas J. and Rita Curtis, "The Local Fiscal Effects of Growth and Commercial Development Over Time," *Urban Land* (Urban Land Institute, January 1993) pp. 18-21.

3. DuPage County Development Department, Planning Division, *Impacts of Development on DuPage County Property Taxes* (Planning Division, Du Page Co., Illinois, October 1991).

4. Stone, Deborah, *Tax Policy: The Rules of the Regional Development Game* (Chicago, Illinois: Metropolitan Planning Council, January 1995). This brief report summarizes the findings of a report commissioned jointly by the MPC and the Federal Reserve Bank of Chicago titled, *Does Business Development Raise Taxes: An Empirical Analysis*, by William H. Oakland, Tulane University, and William A. Testa, Federal Reserve Bank of Chicago, (January 1995).

5. Logan, John R. and Harvey L. Molotch, *Urban Fortunes: The Political Economy of Place* (Berkeley: University of California Press, 1987).

6. Molotch, Harvey, "The City as a Growth Machine: Toward a Political Economy of Place," *American Journal of Sociology*, vol. 82 (2) (1976).

7. Bartlett, Albert A., "Reflections on Sustainability, Population Growth, and the Environment," *Population and Environment: A Journal of Interdisciplinary Studies*, 16 (1) (24 September 1994).

8. Freudenburg, William R., "A Good Business Climate as Bad Economic News?" *Society and Natural Resources*, 3 (1990) pp. 313-31.

9. Landis, John D., "Do Growth Controls Work? An Evaluation of Local Growth Control Programs in Seven California Cities," *CPS Brief* (Berkeley: California Policy Seminar) 4 (2) (1992).

10. Glickfeld, Madelyn and Ned Levine, *Regional Growth ... Local Reaction* (Cambridge, Massachusetts: Lincoln Institute of Land Use Policy, 1992).

11. This data was developed by Coalition for a Livable Future in Portland, Oregon and appeared in *The Oregonian*, 22 December 1996.

12. Cannon, Frederick, "Economic Growth and the Environment", *Economic & Business Outlook*, (Bank of America, June/July 1993).

13. Meyer, Stephen M., Environmentalism and Economic Prosperity: An Update (Cambridge, Massachusetts: Massachusetts Institute of Technology, Project on Environmental Politics and Policy, 1993). This paper updates the report *Environmentalism and Economic Prosperity: Testing the Environmental Impact Hypothesis*, 1992.

14. Hall, Bob, *Gold & Green Index* (Durham, North Carolina: Institute for Southern Studies, Fall 1994).

15. Templet, Paul H. "The Emissions-to-Jobs Ratio," *Environmental Science and Technology*, vol. 27(5) (1993) pp. 810-12. Templet is an associate professor at Louisiana State University for Environmental Studies. He has a Masters degree in physical chemistry from Duke University and a Ph.D. in chemical physics from LSU.

16. Oregon Business Council, *Oregon Values and Beliefs, Study Summary* (May 1993).

17. Berry, Sandra H., *Los Angeles Today and Tomorrow: Results of the Los Angeles 2000 Community Survey* (Rand Corporation, October 1988). The survey polled 1,230 of the city's residents on a range of issues. A preference for slowing/stopping growth existed in all racial and ethnic

categories. The survey also found that 85 percent of respondents supported development impact fees as their preferred revenue source.

18. *The Colorado Looks At Growth Survey* was conducted in January 1995 for the Colorado Smart Growth and Development Summit by Talmey-Drake Research & Strategy, Inc., of Boulder, Colorado. The results of the survey are based on 2,223 random telephone interviews with adult Colorado residents. The margin of error for weighted statewide results is plus or minus three percent.

19. Daly, Herman E., "Sustainable Growth? No Thank You," in Mander, Jerry and Edward Goldsmith, eds., *The Case Against the Global Economy and for a Turn Toward the Local* (San Francisco: Sierra Club Books, 1996).

20. Cobb, Clifford, Ted Halstead and Jonathan Rowe, "Genuine Progress Indicator: Summary of Data and Methodology," Fig.1, *Redefining Progress* (San Francisco, California: 1995).

21. American Farmland Trust, "Frederick County Cost of Community Services Study," *American Farmland* (spring-summer 1997).

22. Auger, Philip A., "Does Open Space Pay?" (Durham, New Hampshire: University of New Hampshire Cooperative Extension, 1995).

23. Cornell, Mark R., Jane H. Lilldabl and Larry D. Singell, "The Effects of Greenbelts on Residential Property Value: Some Findings on the Political Economy of Open Space," *Land Economics* vol. 54 (2) (1978).

24. Reilly, William K, "Across the Barricades," *Land Use In America* (1996) p. 189.

4. The Truth About Jobs, Housing, and Growth

1. Henry David Thoreau cited by Hayden, Dolores, *Redesigning the American Dream: The Future of Housing, Work and Family* (W.W. Norton, 1984) p. 39.

2. Rufolo, Anthony M., and J. O'Shea Gumusoglu, *Literature Review of Business Development Tax Incentives*, prepared for the Oregon Department of Economic Development (April 1995).

3. Bartik, Timothy J., "Who Benefits from Local Job Growth, Migrants or the Original Residents?" *Regional Studies* vol. 27 (4) (1993) pp. 297-311.

4. Templet, Paul H. and Stephen Farber, "The Complementarity Between Environmental and Economic Risk: An Empirical Analysis," *Ecological Economics* vol. 9 (1994) pp. 153-65.

5. *The State of Small Business: A Report to the President* (Washington, D.C.: U.S. Small Business Administration, 1992). This report says "from 1988 to 1990, small firms have created all of the net new jobs in the economy and most this growth has occurred in firms with fewer than 20 employees." Later in the report (p. 44) it says "92 percent of small-

firm jobs were created by firms with fewer than 20 employees."

6. Johnson, Robin, Housing Consultant, "Inclusionary Housing Programs," memorandum, City of Eugene Planning and Development Department, Eugene, Oregon, 31 January 1995.

5. DISCOVERING THE REAL COST OF GROWTH IN YOUR COMMUNITY

1. Real Estate Research Corporation, *The Cost of Sprawl*, prepared for the Council on Environmental Quality, U.S. Government Printing Office, April 1974.
2. American Farmland Trust, *Density-Related Public Costs* (Washington, D.C.: 1986).
3. See related discussion of Myth 10 in Chapter 3. See also American Farmland Trust, *Does Farmland Protection Pay? The Cost of Community Services in Three Massachusetts Towns* (Northampton, Massachusetts: 1992); and their most recent, "Frederick County [Maryland] Cost of Community Services Study," in *American Farmland* (spring-summer 1997).
4. Economic and Planning Systems, Inc., *Phase 2 Report: Cost of Growth Model — Baseline Forecast and Case Studies* (City of Redmond: April 1997).
5. American Farmland Trust, *Alternatives for Future Urban Growth in California's Central Valley: The Bottom Line for Agriculture and Taxpayers*, Summary Report (Davis, California: October 1995).
6. Burchell, Robert W., et al. *Impact Assessment of the New Jersey Interim State Development and Redevelopment Plan* (Center for Urban Policy Research, Rutgers University, for New Jersey Office of State Planning: February 1992).
7. Burchell, Robert W., *Fiscal Impacts of Alternative Land Development Patterns in Michigan: The Cost of Current Development Versus Compact Growth* (Southeast Michigan Council of Governments: March 1997).
8. Burchell, Robert W., et al., *Cost of Sprawl Revisited: The Evidence of Sprawl's Negative and Positive Impacts* (Washington, D.C.: National Transportation Research Board and National Research Council, 1998). A comprehensive literature review.
9. DuPage County Development Dept., *Impacts of Development on DuPage County Property Taxes*, prepared for the County Regional Planning Commission (Illinois: October 1991).
10. Stone, Deborah, *Tax Policy: The Rules of the Regional Development Game* (Chicago, Illinois: Metropolitan Planning Council, January 1995). This brief report summarized the findings of a report commissioned jointly by the MPC and the Federal Reserve Bank of Chicago: *Does Business Development Raise Taxes: An Empirical Analysis*, by

William H. Oakland, Tulane University, and William A. Testa, Federal Reserve Bank of Chicago (January 1995).

11. Santa Fe City Planning Department, *Growth Impact Study* (Santa Fe, New Mexico: 1973).

12. Springfield Planning Department, *The Cost of Growth: 1971-1981* (Springfield, Oregon).

13. Refer to: Frank, James E., *The Cost of Alternative Development Patterns: A Review of the Literature* (Washington, D.C.: Urban Land Institute, 1989); Nicholas, James C., Arthur C. Nelson and Julian C. Juergensmeyer, *A Practitioner's Guide to Development Impact Fees*, (Chicago, Illinois: APA Planners Press, 1991); and Office of Planning and Research, *Paying the Piper: New Ways to Pay for Public Infrastructure in California* (Sacramento, California: December 1982).

14. Fodor, Eben V., "The Real Cost of Growth in Oregon," *Population & Environment*, vol. 18 (March 1997).

15. Tischler and Associates, Inc., *Development Excise Tax* (Boulder, Colorado: 29 July 1996).

16. Burchell, Robert W., David Listokin and William R. Dolphin, *Development Impact Assessment Handbook* (Washington, D.C.: Urban Land Institute, 1994).

17. Burchell, Robert W., *Impact Assessment of the New Jersey Interim State Development and Redevelopment Plan.*

18. Eugene Water and Electric Board, *EWEB System Development Charge: Methodology and Rate Structure Proposal* (Eugene, Oregon: 5 July 1996).

19. Santa Barbara Planning Task Force, *Santa Barbara: The Impacts of Growth — Citywide Effects*, vol.1 (1974).

20. Thurston Regional Planning Council, *Financing Region-Wide Infrastructure Report, 1997-2002* (September 1997).

6. PUTTING THE BRAKES ON GROWTH — WHAT WORKS?

1. This example is from P.C. Putnam as quoted by Carlo M. Cipolla, *The Economic History of World Population*, 7th ed. (Penguin Books, 1978).

2. Bartlett, Albert A., *Boulder Tomorrow?*

3. Northwest Public Policy Research Program, *The Mind of Colorado: A 1995 Statewide Survey* (University of Colorado, Denver: 1995).

4. ECO Northwest, *Evaluation of No-Growth and Slow-Growth Policies for the Portland Region* (Portland, Oregon: Metro, June 1994) p. B-3.

5. Survey by Conservation Voters of Oregon (Portland), 1996.

6. Glickfeld, Madelyn and Ned Levine, *Regional Growth ... Local Reaction* (Cambridge, Massachusetts: Lincoln Institute of Land Use Policy, 1992).

7. Ibid.

8. Templet, Paul H. and Stephen Farber, "The Complementarity Between Environmental and Economic Risk: An Empirical Analysis," *Ecological Economics*, vol. 9 (1994) pp. 153-65.

9. Former Colorado governor Richard Lamm was quoted in the 23 April 1997 edition of *The Christian Science Montor*: "What really scares me is that we seem to be growing a Los Angeles of the Rockies."

10. See website http://tis-nt.eh.doe.gov/nepa/policy/policy.htm.

11. Ruane, Eugene T. and Robert J. Gray, *Community Response to Population Growth and Environmental Stress: A National Inventory of Local Growth Management Strategies* (Washington, D.C.: Population-Environment Balance, July 1987).

12. Wackernagel, Mathis and William Rees, *Our Ecological Footprint: Reducing Human Impact on the Earth* (Gabriola Island, B.C.: New Society Publishers, 1996).

13. This study was reported in Diamond, Henry L. and Partick F. Noonan, *Land Use in America* (Washington, D.C.: Island Press, 1996) p. 36.

14. Livingston, Laurence and John A. Blayney, *Foothill Environmental Design Study: Open Space vs. Development*, final report to the City of Palo Alto (1971).

15. Smith, R., L. Propst and W. Abberger, *Local Land Acquisition for Conservation: Trends and Facts to Consider* (Washington, D.C.: World Wildlife Fund, 1991).

16. Brighton, Deb, Ad Hoc Associates, Salisbury, Vermont, *Likely Tax Consequences of Conservation or Development of Mack Orchards*, Londonderry, New Hampshire, prepared for Trust for Public Land, Boston, Massachusetts (February, 1996).

17. Feder, Barnaby J. "Towns Are Slowing Invasion of Farms by Bulldozers," *New York Times* (March 20, 1997).

18. Fishman P. Richard, "Public Land Banking: Examination of a Management Technique;" and Sylvan Kamm, "The Realities of Large Scale Public Land Banking," *Management and Control of Growth*, vol. III (Washington, D.C.: Urban Land Institute, 1975).

19. Santa Barbara Planning Task Force, *Santa Barbara: The Impacts of Growth – Citywide Effects*, vol. 1 (1974).

7. THE NEW MILLENIUM COMMUNITY

1. Daly, Herman E., *Steady-State Economics*, 2nd Ed. (Washington, D.C.: Island Press, 1991).

2. Ibid.

3. Bartlett, Albert A., "Reflections on Sustainability, Population Growth, and the Environment," *Population and Environment: A Journal of Interdisciplinary Studies*, vol. 16 (1) (24 September 1994).

4. Daly, Herman E., *Steady-State Economics*, 2nd Ed. (Washington, D.C.:

Island Press, 1991).

5. Ibid.

6. Clark, Mary E., *Ariande's Thread: The Search for New Modes of Thinking*, (New York: St. Martin's Press, 1989) tab. 16.1.

7. Minnesota Sustainable Development Initiative, *Challenges for a Sustainable Minnesota: A Minnesota Strategic Plan for Sustainable Development* (St Paul: Minnesota Environmental Quality Board, July 1995).

APPENDIX A: SELECTED REFERENCES ON URBAN GROWTH

This section is organized under the following topic headings:

- Growth Management
- Cost of Growth
- Development Impact Fees
- Growth and the Economy
- Growth Politics
- Community Planning Tools
- Valuing Open Space
- Sustainability, Land Use, and Miscellaneous

References marked with one asterick (*) are recommended and those marked with two astericks are highly recommended

GROWTH MANAGEMENT

Note: These growth management publications are the best available in the planning literature. However, as noted in the text, much of the official planning literature is pessimistic about growth management as a means of slowing growth. This pessimism may be premature given the relatively early and still experimental nature of growth management in the U.S.

DeGrove, John M., *Emerging State and Regional Roles in Growth Management* (Cambridge, Massachusetts: Lincoln Institute of Land Policy, July 1992).

Duerksen, Chris, Erin Johnson, and Cheryl Fricke of Clarion Associates, *Colorado Growth Management Toolbox* (Appendix to Smart Growth and Development Summit White Paper) January, 1995. Report available on the web at <www.state.co.us/smartgrowth/>*

ECO Northwest, *Evaluation of No-Growth and Slow-Growth Policies for the Portland Region* (Portland, Oregon: Metro, June 1994). While serving as a useful technical reference, this publication does not provide any recommendations for actually slowing or stopping growth, as its title would imply.

Glickfeld, Madelyn and Ned Levine, *Regional Growth ... Local Reaction: The Enactment and Effects of Local Growth Control and Management Measures in California* (Cambridge, Massachusetts: Lincoln Institute of Land Policy, 1992). *

Kelly, Eric Damian, *Planning, Growth, and Public Facilities: A Primer for Local Officials*, Planning Advisory Service Report No. 447 (Chicago, Illinois: American Planning Association, 1993).

Landis, John D., "Do Growth Controls Work? An Evaluation of Local Growth Control Programs in Seven California Cities," *CPS Brief* (California Policy Seminar, Berkeley, CA), vol. 4 (2) (1992).*

Mantell, Micheal A., Stephen F. Harper, and Luther Propst, *Creating Successful Communities: A Guidebook to Growth Management Strategies* (The Conservation Foundation, Island Press, 1990). *

Miness, Deborah and Robert C. Einsweiler, *Bibliography on Academic and Professional Literature on Growth and Growth Management* (Cambridge, Massachusetts: Lincoln Institute of Land Policy, 1992).

Nelson, Arthur C. and James B. Duncan, *Growth Management Principles & Practices*, Chicago, Illinois: Planners Press, American Planners Association, 1995). An excellent and readable reference for getting acquainted with growth management as it is being practiced today.*

Porter, Douglas R., ed., *Growth Management: Keeping on Target?* (Urban Land Institute and Lincoln Institute of Land Policy, 1986).

____, *Managing Growth in America's Communities*, (Washington, D.C.: Island Press, 1997). *

____, ed., *Performance Standards for Growth Management*, Planning Advisory Service Report No. 461 (American Planning Association, February 1996).

Ruane, Eugene T. and Robert J. Gray, *Community Response to Population Growth and Environmental Stress: A National Inventory of Local Growth Management Strategies* (Washington, D.C.: Population-Environment Balance, July 1987).

Santa Barbara Planning Task Force, *Santa Barbara: The Impacts of Growth — Citywide Effects*, vol. 1 (1974). One of the most impressive reports written on growth impacts. Compiled entirely by a volunteer citizen task force with the support of the city. Still available from the city's planning department for $20. **

Schiffman, Irving, *Alternative Techniques for Managing Growth* (Institute of Government Studies, University of California at Berkeley, 1989).

Useful, but focused mostly on planning for growth and less on restraining growth.

Stein, Jay M., ed., *Growth Management: The Planning Challenge of the 1990's* (Newbury Park, California: Sage Publications, 1993).

Urban Land Institute, *Management & Control of Growth — Issues, Techniques, Problems, Trends*, vol. I, II, III (Washington, D.C.:1975). A very impressive early collection of hundreds of essays, reports, and analyses on the full range of growth issues. Too technical and dated for most readers.

COSTS OF GROWTH

American Farmland Trust, *Alternatives for Future Urban Growth in California's Central Valley: The Bottom Line for Agriculture and Taxpayers*, Summary Report (Davis, California October, 1995).

American Farmland Trust, *Density-Related Public Costs* (Washington, D.C., 1986). **

Bank of America, *Beyond Sprawl: New Patterns of Growth to Fit the New California* (January 1995). Contact BoA Environmental Policies and Programs, No. 5800, P.O. Box 37000, San Francisco, CA 94137; Phone: 415-622-8154.

Black, Thomas J. and Rita Curtis, "The Local Fiscal Effects of Growth and Commercial Development Over Time", *Urban Land* (Urban Land Institute, January 1993) pp. 18—21.

Bucknall, Christopher P., *The Real Cost of Development* (Poughkeepsie, New York: Scenic Hudson Inc, 1990).

Burchell, Robert W., *Fiscal Impacts of Alternative Land Development Patterns in Michigan: The Cost of Current Development Versus Compact Growth* (Southeast Michigan Council of Governments, March 1997). The most recent comprehensive study showing the high public costs associated with sprawling development.

Burchell, Robert W., et al., *Cost of Sprawl Revisited: The Evidence of Sprawl's Negative and Positive Impacts* (Washington, D.C.: National Transportation Research Board and National Research Council, 1998). A comprehensive literature review. *

_____, *Development Impact Assessment Handbook* (Washington, D.C:. Urban Land Institute, 1994).*

_____, *Impact Assessment of the New Jersey Interim State Development and Redevelopment Plan* (Center for Urban Policy Research, Rutgers University for New Jersey Office of State Planning, February 1992).

_____, *The New Practitioner's Guide to Fiscal Impact Analysis* (Piscataway, New Jersey: Center for Urban Policy Research, Rutgers University, 1985).

Coalition for Smarter Growth, *Highway Robbery* (October 1997). A report on the high costs and potential subsidies involved in proposals to expand roads in the Washington, D.C. area. Coalition phone: 202-588-5570; email: stopsprawl@aol.com.

DuPage County Development Department, *Impacts of Development on DuPage County Property Taxes*, prepared for the County Regional Planning Commission, Illinois (October 1991).*

Fodor, Eben V., "The Real Cost of Growth in Oregon", *Population & Environment* vol. 18 (March 1997).

Frank, James E., *The Cost of Alternative Development Patterns: A Review of the Literature* (Washington, D.C.: Urban Land Institute, 1989).*

Ladd, Helen F., "Population Growth, Density and the Costs of Providing Public Services", *Urban Studies*, vol. 29 (April 1992) pp. 273-95.

Nelson, Arthur C., "Development Impact Fees," *Journal of the American Planning Association*, vol. 54 (Winter 1988) pp.3-6.

Office of Planning and Research, *Paying the Piper: New Ways to Pay for Public Infrastructure in California* (Sacramento, California: December 1982).

Piedmont Environmental Council, *Taxes and Growth in Loudoun County* (Warrenton, Virginia: 1993).

Real Estate Research Corporation, *The Cost of Sprawl*, prepared for the Council on Environmental Quality (U. S. Government Printing Office: April 1974). This is the classic, widely quoted study on the cost of sprawl. *

Sierra Club, *Sprawl Costs Us All — A Sierra Club Report* (September 1997). An excellent summary of urban sprawl issues as they affect the state of Virginia. Available for $5 from Sierra Club Foundation, c/o Regional Office, 69 Franklin Street, Annapolis, Maryland 21401; Phone: 410-268-7411.

Springfield Planning Department, *The Cost of Growth: 1971-1981* (June 1982). Contact: 225 5th St., Springfield, Oregon 97477; Phone: 541-726-3778.

Vance, Tamara A., Arthur B. Larson, *Fiscal Impact of Major Land Uses in Culpeper County Virginia* (Warrenton, Virginia: Piedmont Environmental Council, February 1988).

DEVELOPMENT IMPACT FEES

Barnebey, Mark P., Tom MacRostie, et al., "Paying for Growth: Community Approaches to Development Impact Fees", *Journal of the American Planning Association* (winter 1988) pp. 18-28.

Bauman, Gus and William Ethier, "Development Exactions and Impact Fees: A Survey of American Practices", *Law and Contemporary Problems* (winter 1987).

Florida Advisory Council on Intergovernmental Relations, *Impact Fees in Florida* (Tallahassee, Florida: November 1986).

Florida Advisory Council on Intergovernmental Relations, *Impact Fees in*

Florida: An Update (Tallahassee, Florida: July 1989).

Jackson, Timothy T., "Traffic Impact Study and Proportionate Stare Impact Fees," *ITE Journal*, vol. 64 (September 1994) pp. 47-51.

Leitner, Martin L. and Eric J. Strauss, "Elements of a Municipal Impact Fee Ordinance, with Commentary," *American Planning Association Journal* (spring 1988) pp. 225-31.

Lillydahl, Jane H., Arthur C. Nelson, et al., "The Need for a Standard State Impact Fee Enabling Act", *Journal of the American Planning Association* (winter 1988) pp. 7-17. *

Nelson, Arthur C. Ed., *Development Impact Fees: Policy Rationale, Practice, Theory, and Issues* (Chicago, Illinois: APA Planners Press, 1988).

Nicholas, James C., Arthur C. Nelson, and Julian C. Juergensmeyer, *A Practitioner's Guide to Development Impact Fees* (Chicago, Illinois: APA Planners Press, 1991). **

Nicholas, James C., "On the Progression of Impact Fees", *Journal of the American Planning Association*, vol. 58 (Autumn 1992) pp. 517-25.

Salkin, Patricia E., *Impact Fees for New York Municipalities: Time for Legislative Action?* (Government Law Center, May 1991). *

Sandler, Ralph D. and Edward T. Denham, *Transportation Impact Fees: The Florida Experience*, presentation at the Transportation Research Board, (January 1986).

Snyder, Thomas P. and Michael A. Stegman, *Paying for Growth: Using Development Impact Fees to Finance Infrastructure* (Urban Land Institute, 1987).

Stroud, Nancy, "Legal Considerations of Development Impact Fees", *Journal of the American Planning Association* (winter 1988) pp. 28-37.

GROWTH AND THE ECONOMY

Cannon, Frederick, Bank of America, "Economic Growth and the Environment", *Economic and Business Outlook* (June/July 1993).

Chesapeake Bay Foundation, *A Dollars and Sense Partnership: Economic Development and Environmental Protection* (Annapolis, Maryland: January 1996). Contact by phone: 410-268-8816. *

Cobb, Clifford, Ted Halstead and Jonathan Rowe, "Genuine Progress Indicator: Summary of Data and Methodology," *Redefining Progress* (San Francisco, Cailifornia: 1995).

Daly, Herman E., *Beyond Growth: The Economics of Sustainable Development* (Boston, Massachusetts: Beacon Press, 1996).

Daly, Herman E., *Steady-State Economics*, 2nd ed. (Washington, D.C.: Island Press, 1991). *

Fodor, Eben V., "The Three Myths of Growth," *Planning Commissioners Journal*, vol. 23 (winter 1996). <www.webcom.com/pcj/articles/fod1>

Freudenburg, William R., "A Good Business Climate as Bad Economic News?," *Society and Natural Resources*, vol. 3 (1990) pp. 313-31. *

Meyer, Stephen M., *Environmentalism and Economic Prosperity: An Update* (Cambridge,Massachusetts: Institute of Technology, Project on Environmental Politics and Policy, Cambridge, February 1993). This paper updates the report *Environmentalism and Economic Prosperity: Testing the Environmental Impact Hypothesis* (1992). *

Power, T. M., *The Economic Value of Quality of Life* (Boulder, Colorado: Westview Press, 1980).

Institute for Southern Studies, *Gold & Green Index* (Durham, North Carolina: fall 1994).

Rufolo, Anthony M. and J. O'Shea Gumusoglu, *Literature Review of Business Development Tax Incentives*, prepared for the Oregon Department of Economic Development (April 1995).

Templet, Paul H., "The Emissions-to-Jobs Ratio", *Environmental Science and Technology*, vol. 27 (5) (1993) pp. 810-12.

Templet, Paul H. and Stephen Farber, "The Complementarity Between Environmental and Economic Risk: An Empirical Analysis", *Ecological Economics*, vol. 9 (1994) pp. 153-65.

GROWTH POLITICS

Molotch, Harvey, "The Political Economy of Growth Machines," *Journal of Urban Affairs*, vol. 15 (1) (1993).

Molotch, Harvey, "The City as a Growth Machine: Toward a Political Economy of Place," *American Journal of Sociology*, vol. 82 (2) (1976) pp. 309-30. **

Logan, John R. and Harvey L. Molotch, *Urban Fortunes: The Political Economy of Place* (Berkeley: University of California Press, 1987).*

COMMUNITY PLANNING TOOLS

Ames, Steven, ed., *A Guide to Community Visioning* (APA Planners Press, 1993). *

Community Environmental Council, *Sustainable Community Indicators: Guideposts for Local Planning*. Available at <www.grc.org/cec/pubs3html> or contact CEC in Santa Barbara, California; phone: 805-963-0583.

Aberley, Doug, ed., *Futures by Design: The Practice of Ecological Planning* (Gabriola Island, British Columbia: New Society Publishers, 1994).

Hart, Maureen, *Guide to Sustainable Community Indicators*, (Ipswich, Massachusetts: QLF/Atlantic Center for the Environment, May 1995) Phone: 508-356-0038.*

Jones, Bernie, *Neighborhood Planning: A Guide for Citizens and Planners* (APA Planning Advisory Service, 1990).

Land Trust Alliance, *Model Conservation Easement and Historic Preservation Easement*, (Washington, D.C.: 1996).

National Recreation and Park Association, *Park, Recreation, Open Space and Greenway Guidelines* (1996). Gives the amount of parkland required to adequately serve various population levels.

Redefining Progress, *The Community Indicators Handbook*. Contact One Kearny Street, 4th Floor, San Francisco, CA 94108; phone: 415-781-1191; Email: info@rprogress.org.

Smith, Herbert H., *The Citizen's Guide to Planning* (APA Planners Press, 1993). Basics of urban planning, zoning, and land regulation.

VALUING OPEN SPACE

American Farmland Trust, *Does Farmland Protection Pay? The Cost of Community Services in Three Massachusetts Towns* (Northampton Massachusetts, 1992).

American Farmland Trust, "Frederick County [Maryland] Cost of Community Services Study,, *American Farmland* (spring-summer 1997).

American Farmland Trust, *Is Farmland Protection a Community Investment? — How to Do a Cost of Community Services Study* (Washington, D.C.: 1993). This step-by-step handbook will tell you how to evaluate the cost of community services for various land uses in your city or county. *

Auger, Philip A., *Does Open Space Pay?* (Durham, New Hampshire: University of New Hampshire Cooperative Extension, 1995).

Brighton, Deb, Ad Hoc Associates, Salisbury, Vermount, *Likely Tax Consequences of Conservation or Development of Mack Orchards* (Londonderry, New Hampshire, prepared for Trust for Public Land, Boston, Massachusetts, February, 1996).

Correll, Mark R., Jane H. Lillydahl, and Larry D. Singell, "The Effects of Greenbelts on Residential Property Values: Some Findings on the Political Economy of Open Space,, *Land Economics*, vol. 54 (1978) pp. 204-17.

Hammer, Thomas R., Robert E. Coghlin, and Edward T. Horn IV, "Research Report: The Effects of a Large Park on Real Estate Value", *Journal of the American Institute of Planners* (July 1974).

Livingston, Laurence and John A. Blayney, *Foothill Environmental Design Study: Open Space vs. Development*, Final Report to the City of Palo Alto, (1971).

Smith, R., L. Propst and W. Abberger, *Local Land Acquisition for Conservation: Trends and Faxts to Consider* (Washington, D.C.: World Wildlife Fund, 1991).

Sonoran Institute, *The Fiscal and Economic Impacts of Local Conservation and Community Development Measures: A Review of the Literature*, (Tuscon, Arizona: February, 1993). Commissioned by the Greater Yellowstone Coalition, Phone: 406-586-1593 **

Thomas, Holly L., *The Economic Benefits of Land Conservation* (Poughkeepsie, New York: Tech Memo, Dutchess County Planning Department, February 1991). *

SUSTAINABILITY, LAND USE, AND MISCELLANEOUS

Bartlett, Albert A., "Reflections on Sustainability, Population Growth, and the Environment," *Population and Environment: A Journal of Interdisciplinary Studies*, vol. 16 (September 1994).*

Bartlett, Albert A., *Arithmetic, Population and Energy.* (video). Contact: University of Colorado Television, Boulder, Colorado, phone: 303-492-1857. A timeless classic and must-see primer on exponential growth based on *The Forgotten Fundamental of the Energy Crisis,* 2nd ed. **

Bartlett, Albert A., *The Mythology of Population Growth* (video). Contact: Educational Communication Inc., Los Angeles, California; Phone: 310-559-9160. Professor Bartlett discusses population growth and the problems it creates in our cities. **

Bartlett, Albert A., "The Arithmetic of Growth: Methods of Calculation", *Population & Environment,* vol. 14 (March 1993) pp. 359-87. This is a tutorial on how to calculate rates of growth from data.

Bartlett, Albert A., "Is there a Population Problem?", *Wild Earth,* vol. 7 (fall 1997) pp. 88-90. This shows that the world's worst population problem is right here in the U.S.

Diamond, Henry L. and Partick F. Noonan, *Land Use in America* (Washington, D.C.: Island Press, 1996).*

Knaap, Gerrit and Arthur C. Nelson, *The Regulated Landscape: Lessons on State Land Use Planning from Oregon* (Lincoln Institute of Land Policy, 1992).

Krizek, Kevin J. and Joe Power, *A Planner's Guide to Sustainable Development* (APA Planning Advisory Service Report No. 467, 1996). A good summary of sustainability concepts and criteria applicable to community planning. *

Reilly, William K., ed., *The Use of Land: A Citizen's Policy Guide to Urban Growth* (1973). A landmark publication heralding a "new mood" in American land use policy.

Roseland, Mark, *Toward Sustainable Communities:Resources for Citizens and Their Governments* (Gabriola Island, B.C.: New Society Publishers, 1998).

The Urban Ecologist. Contact: 405 14th Street, Suite 701, Oakland, CA 94612. The group, Urban Ecology, developed the *Sustainable City Plan* for Berkeley in 1992.

Wackernagel, Mathis and William Rees, *Our Ecological Footprint: Reducing Human Impact on the Earth* (Gabriola Island, B.C.: New Society Publishers, 1996). *

Note: To obtain American Planning Association publications or to request their publication catalog, write to APA, 122 S. Michigan Avenue, Suite 1600, Chicago, IL 60603 or phone: 312-786-6344.

Appendix B: Organizations Concerned with Land Use

NATIONAL AND GLOBAL

American Farmland Trust
1920 N Street N.W., Suite 400
Washington, D.C. 20036
Phone: 202-659-5170
Fax: 202-659-8339
Email: info@farmland.org

American Planning Association
122 South Michigan Ave., Suite 1600
Chicago, IL 60603
Phone: 312-431-9100
Fax: 312-431-9985
Email: PublicInfo@planning.org

Canadian Nature Federation
1 Nicholas Street, Suite 606
Ottawa, Ontario
Canada K1N 7B7
Email: CNF@cnf.ca.
<www.magma.ca/~cnfgen/>

Canadian Parks and Wilderness Society
Suite 380, 401 Richmond Street W.
Toronto, Ontario
Canada M5V 3A8
Phone: 416-979-2720
Fax: 416-979-3155
Email: cpaws@icomm.ca

Carrying Capacity Network
2000 P Street, N.W., Suite 240
Washington, D.C. 20036
Phone: 202-296-4548
Fax: 202-296-4609
Email: CCN@igc.apc.org

Earth Island Institute
300 Broadway, Suite 28
San Francisco, CA 94133-3312
Email: earthisland@earthisland.org
Phone: 415-788-3666 Ext. 123
Fax: 415-788-7324
<www.earthisland.org/ei/>

Friends of the Earth
1025 Vermont Ave., N.W., 3rd Floor
Washington, D.C. 20005-6303
Phone: 202-783-7400
Fax: 202-783-0444
Email: foe@foe.org
<www/foe.org>

The Growth Management Institute
5406 Trent Street
Chevy Chase, MD 20815
Phone/Fax: 301-656-9560
Email: dporter@gmionline.org

The Land Trust Alliance
1319 F Street, N.W., Suite 501
Washington, D.C. 20004
Phone: 202-638-4725
Fax: 202-638-4730
<www.lta.org/www_lta_.html>

Lincoln Institute of Land Policy
113 Brattle Street
Cambridge, MA 02138-3400
Phone: 617-661-3016
Fax: 617-661-7235
<www.lincolninst.edu/lincoln>

National Audubon Society
Population & Habitat Campaign
3109 28th Street
Boulder, CO 80301
Phone: 303-442-2600
Fax: 303-442-2199 fax

**National Growth Management
Leadership Project**
716 Willamette Building
534 SW Third Avenue
Portland, OR 97204
Phone: 503-228-9462

**National Trust for Historic
Preservation**
1785 Massachusetts Avenue N.W.
Washington, D.C. 20036
Phone: 202-588-6000

Fax: 202-588-6038

**Natural Resources Defense
Council**
40 West 20th Street
New York, NY 10011
Phone: 212-727-2700
<www.nrdc.org/nrdc/>

New Road Map Foundation
P.O. Box 15981
Seattle, WA 98115-0981
Phone: 206-527-0437

Northwest Environment Watch
1402 Third Avenue, Suite 1127
Seattle, WA 98101-2118
Phone: 206-447-1880, 888-643-9820
Email: new@northwestwatch.org
<www.northwestwatch.org>

Population-Environment Balance
2000 P Street N.W., Suite 210
Washington, D.C. 20036-5909
Phone: 202-955-5700
Fax: 202-955-6161
Email: uspop@balance.org/

Sierra Club
85 Second Street, Second Floor
San Francisco, CA 94105-3441
Phone: 415-977-5500
Fax: 415-977-5799
Email: information@sierraclub.org

**Trust for Public Land
(National Office)**
116 New Montgomery, 4th Floor
San Francisco, CA 94105

Phone: 415-495-4014
Fax: 415-495-4103
Email: mailbox@tpl.org
<www.igc.apc.org/tpl/>

The Urban Land Institute (emphasis on real estate development)
1025 Thomas Jefferson Street, N.W., Suite 500W
Washington D.C. 20007-5201
Phone: 202-624-7000
Fax: 202-624-7140

The Wilderness Society
900 17th Street, N.W.
Washington, D.C. 20006

World Resources Institute
1709 New York Avenue, 7th Floor
Washington, D.C. 20006
Phone: 202-638-6300
Fax: 202-638-0036
Email: lauralee@wri.org.

Worldwatch Institute
1776 Massachusetts Avenue, N.W.
Washington, D.C. 20036-1904
Phone: 202-452-1999
Fax: 202-296-7365
Email: worldwatch@worldwatch.org

The York Centre for Applied Sustainability (formerly The National Roundtable on the Environment and the Economy)
c/o Faculty of Environmental Studies,

355 Lumbers Building, York University,
4700 Keele Street, Downsview
Ontario, Canada M3J 1P3
Phone: 416-736-5285
Fax: 416-736-5679
<www.YorkU.CA/faculty/fes/ycas/>

U.S. STATE AND REGIONAL

CALIFORNIA
Greenbelt Alliance
530 Bush Street, Suite 303
San Francisco, CA 94108
Phone: 415-398-3730
Fax: 415-398-6530

COLORADO
Colorado Environmental Coalition
2323 20th Street
Boulder, CO 80304
Phone: 303-443-5931
Fax: 303-443-2729

FLORIDA
1000 Friends of Florida, Inc.
P.O. Box 5948
Tallahassee, FL 32314
Phone: 904-222-6277
Fax: 904-222-1117

GEORGIA
The Georgia Conservancy
1776 Peachtree Street, N.W.
Suite 400 South
Atlanta, GA 30309
Phone: 404-876-2900
Fax: 404-872-9229
Email: tgc@atlanta.com

HAWAII
Hawaii's Thousand Friends
305 Hahani Street, Suite 282
Kailuah, HI 96734
Phone: 808-262-0682
Fax: 808-262-0682

ILLINOIS
Openlands Project
220 South State Street, Suite 1880
Chicago, IL 60604
Phone: 312-427-4256
Fax: 312-427-6251
Email: openlands@aol.com

KENTUCKY
Bluegrass Tomorrow
465 E. High Street, Suite 208
Lexington, KY 40507-1941
Phone: 606-259-9829
Fax: 606-259-2743

MAINE
Natural Resources Council of Maine
271 State Street
Augusta, ME 04330
Phone: 207-622-3101
Fax: 207-622-4343

MARYLAND
Chesapeake Bay Foundation
162 Prince George Street
Annapolis, MD 21401
Phone: 410-268-8816
Fax: 410-268-6687

MICHIGAN
Michigan Environmental Council
119 Pere Marquette, Suite 24
Lansing, MI 48912

Phone: 517-487-9539
Fax: 517-487-9541
Email: mienvcouncil@igc.apc.org

MINNESOTA
1000 Friends of Minnesota
2200 Fourth Street
White Bear Lake, MN 55110
Phone: 612-653-0618
Fax: 612-653-0589

MONTANA
Greater Yellowstone Coalition
P.O. Box 1874
Bozeman, MT 59771
Phone: 406-586-1593
Fax: 406-586-0851

NEW JERSEY
New Jersey Future
204 West State Street
Trenton, NJ 08608
Phone: 201-222-6800
Fax: 201-222-6899
Email: njfuture@aol.com

NEW MEXICO
1000 Friends of New Mexico
115 2nd Street, SW
Albuquerque, NM 87102
Phone: 505-848-8232
Fax: 505-242-3964

NEW YORK
Regional Plan Association
61 Broadway, 11th Floor
New York, NY 10006-2701
Phone: 212-785-8000
Fax: 212-785-4816
Email: rpa@maestro.com

NORTH CAROLINA
Western N. Carolina Alliance
P.O. Box 182
Asheville, NC 28802
Phone: 704-254-6484 or 704-258-8737
Fax: 704-253-2188

OHIO
EcoCity Cleveland
2841 Scarborough Road
Cleveland Heights, OH 44118
Phone/Fax: 216-932-3007

OREGON
1000 Friends of Oregon
534 S.W. Third Avenue, Suite 300
Portland, OR 97204
Phone: 503-497-1000
Fax: 503-223-0073

PENNSYLVANIA
**Pennsylvania Environmental
Council**
1211 Chestnut Street, Suite 900
Philadelphia, PA 19107
Phone: 215-563-0250
Fax: 215-563-0528

RHODE ISLAND
Save the Bay, Inc.
434 Smith Street
Providence, RI 02908
Phone: 401-272-3540
Fax: 401-273-7153
Email: savebay@savethebay.org

SOUTH CAROLINA
**The South Carolina Coastal
Conservation League**
456 King Street, P.O. Box 1765
Charleston, SC 29402

Phone: 803-723-8035
Fax: 803-723-8308
Email: scccl@aol.com

VERMONT
**Vermont Natural Resources
Council**
9 Bailey Avenue
Montpelier, VT 05602
Phone: 802-223-2328
Fax: 802-223-0287
Email: vnrc@together.org

VIRGINIA
**The Piedmont Environmental
Council**
P.O. Box 460, 45 Horner Street
Warrenton, VA 20188
Phone: 540-347-2334
Fax: 540-349-9003
Email: pec@mnsic.com
<www.pec-va.org>

WASHINGTON
1000 Friends of Washington
1305 4th Avenue, Suite 303
Seattle, WA 98101
Phone: 206-343-0681
Fax: 206-343-0683

WISCONSIN
1000 Friends of Wisconsin
College of Natural Resources
University of Wisconsin
1900 Franklin Street
Stevens Point, WI 54481
Phone: 715-346-2386
Fax: 715-346-3624

About the Author

Eben Fodor holds a Master of Science degree in Environmental Studies and a Masters in Urban and Regional Planning, both from the University of Oregon. His graduate work focused in the areas of environmental economics, natural resource management, and sustainability. He has a Bachelor's of Science degree in Mechanical Engineering from the University of Wisconsin, Madison.

Fodor founded Friends of Eugene in 1993, a charitable organization created to encourage greater public involvement in local planning and land use issues. He served as president for three years and continues to serve on the board. He is a founding member of Citizens for Public Accountability, a Eugene-area group concerned about the environmental and economic impacts of the Hyundai computer chip factory and the lack of public accountability in local economic development programs. He helped found LandWatch Lane County in 1996 to promote responsible land use policies in the county and serves on the board. He served as executive director of the Community Progress Board — a group of business, civic, and environmental leaders who worked together to develop quality of life and sustainability indicators for the Eugene-Springfield metro area.

Before moving to Oregon, Fodor worked in Washington, D.C. as an engineer and executive in the energy industry developing energy conservation programs and high-efficiency technology for residential and commercial space conditioning. He served as an elected neighborhood leader in Washington, D.C. during one of that area's most rapid growth periods (1987–1990).

He now works primarily as a public interest community planning consultant (i.e., not a development planner) doing land use and growth management consulting, development impact analysis, and sustainable community planning. He has been one of the Northwest's leading researchers on the impacts of urban growth. As an associate with the Institute for a Sustainable Environment at the University of Oregon, he began the Sustainable Communities Project to help Oregon communities begin implementing principles of sustainability. He writes articles on growth and sustainability issues and speaks on these topics across the U.S.

New Society Publishers' mission
is to publish books that contribute in fundamental ways
to building an ecologically sustainable and just society,
and to do so with the least possible impact on the
environment, in a manner that models that vision.

If you have enjoyed *Better NOT Bigger*, you may also find
the following titles to be of interest:

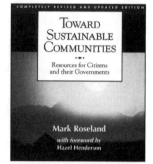

THIS PLACE CALLED HOME	TOWARD SUSTAINABLE COMMUNITIES
Tools for Sustainable Communities — CD-ROM	**Resources for Citizens and Their Governments**
Alliance for Community Education	Mark Roseland
A stimulating resource library of video, still photos, audio, interviews and hundreds of pages of text.	The best resource available on how to apply the concept of sustainable development in communities everywhere.
Mac/WIN	256 pages Illustrations Index
US$24.95 / Can$29.95	US$19.95 / Can$26.95

For a complete catalog, please call 1-800-567-6772, or check out our

on-line catalog at: www.newsociety.com

NSP